TRILBY JAMES

Trilby James read Drama at Bristol University before completing the three-year acting course at RADA. She graduated in 1990 and over the years has worked extensively as an actor in theatre, film and television. In 2000 she also began working as a freelance director and teacher at several leading drama schools including ALRA, Arts Educational Schools, Royal Central School of Speech and Drama, East 15, Mountview Academy of Theatre Arts and the Royal Academy of Dramatic Art where she is now an Associate Teacher. She continues to work across courses, directing third-year performances as well as teaching first and second-year students and running workshops for shorter programmes. She is a script reader and dramaturg for Kali Theatre Company and has directed several play-readings for their 'Talkback' seasons.

THE GOOD AUDITION GUIDES

CLASSICAL MONOLOGUES
edited by Marina Caldarone

CONTEMPORARY MONOLOGUES
edited by Trilby James

SHAKESPEARE MONOLOGUES
edited by Luke Dixon

SHAKESPEARE MONOLOGUES FOR YOUNG PEOPLE
edited by Luke Dixon

The Good Audition Guides

CONTEMPORARY MONOLOGUES FOR MEN

edited and introduced by

TRILBY JAMES

NICK HERN BOOKS
London
www.nickhernbooks.co.uk

A NICK HERN BOOK

The Good Audition Guides:
Contemporary Monologues for Men
first published in Great Britain in 2014
by Nick Hern Books Limited
The Glasshouse, 49a Goldhawk Road, London W12 8QP

Reprinted 2014

Introduction copyright © 2014 Trilby James
Copyright in this selection © 2014 Nick Hern Books Ltd

Designed and typeset by Nick Hern Books, London
Printed and bound by CPI Group (UK) Ltd

A CIP catalogue record for this book
is available from the British Library

ISBN 978 1 85459 563 8

Contents

6

8

Introduction

☞ WHY CONTEMPORARY?

Whether you are still at school auditioning for a youth theatre, about to leave school and want to go to drama school, at drama school looking for showcase material, or a young professional actor preparing for a specific audition, a well-chosen contemporary monologue will be a key component in your audition repertoire. It should reflect something of your own taste and, depending on the style of writing, may provide an opportunity to show something more intimate, more televisual than a classical speech might allow.

The fifty monologues in this volume are from plays that have been written post-2000. With the odd exception the characters range in age from fourteen to thirty-five. There is a wide variety of character types and styles of writing from which to choose. They are all drawn from the extensive list of new plays published by Nick Hern Books.

☞ CHOOSING YOUR MONOLOGUE

I have often likened finding the perfect monologue to finding the perfect pair of jeans. It is rarely a case of 'one size fits all'. You might have to try on several pairs, in different stores, before you find the cut that works for you, but once you have, you will feel confident in the knowledge that you are looking and feeling your best. So it is with audition speeches. You need to find pieces that suit you, that you cannot wait to perform and that will get even better with wear.

If you are auditioning for a youth theatre:

- You will be judged on your potential and your willingness to be open, honest and free. Nobody is looking for a polished or over-rehearsed performance. It is best therefore to choose pieces that allow you to express yourself and for a panel to see something of who you really are.

- Choose something close to you in age and type. Something to which you can relate. Something that inspires you, from a play that speaks to you.

- Avoid accents unless you are really good at them.

If you are auditioning for drama school:

- And have been asked to prepare a classical speech, choose a contemporary monologue that will provide contrast. For example, you may have a Shakespearean monologue that is pensive or tragic so opt for something comic. Similarly, if your classical speech is light in tone, choose something that shows off a more serious side.

If you are already at drama school:

- And you are looking to extend your range, you will want to choose a monologue that stretches you. Perhaps you are studying a particular accent or type of character quite different from yourself.

- And are looking for showcase material, think about how you wish to present yourself. Consider whether you are right for the part you have chosen and whether, if there was to be another production of the play, you could be easily cast in the role.

If you are auditioning for a specific role in a professional production (and have been asked to prepare an additional piece that is not from the play for which you are being seen):

- Choose something close to the part for which you are auditioning.

- Consider the language of the piece and whether you are after something heightened and obviously theatrical or whether you require something more intimate, and realistic.

If you are looking to extend your showreel:

- It may sound obvious, but think about what sort of speeches would be best suited to the varying demands of radio or television.

☞ PREPARING YOUR MONOLOGUE

- Learn your speeches well in advance of the actual audition. Should you forget your lines the panel will be able to tell whether it is out of nervousness or insufficient preparation.

- Read the play. You may be asked questions about it or be required to improvise around it.

- Undertake all necessary research. Make a study of the historical, social and political world of the play. Be sure to understand the meaning of unfamiliar words and references. If the character's accent is not native to you, work hard to perfect it.

- Remain flexible in the way you perform/stage your monologue. Be prepared to be redirected in an audition.

- Using props. There are no hard-and-fast rules about the use of stage properties at an audition. However, common sense suggests that, if you can easily carry an object in your pocket (i.e. a letter, a ring, a handkerchief, etc.), by all means bring this to an audition. If the object to which you refer is large, imagine it is there, or, if necessary, mime using it. Some might even argue that miming props is simpler, and in certain cases much more practical. In any event, you need not worry about being 'marked down' by your decision either to use real objects or to mime using them. What is important is that they do not become burdensome and get in the way of your acting.

- Try not to get stuck in a mode of delivery. It is useful to consider that, unless a character is making a political or after-dinner speech, chances are they have no idea they are going to speak for such a long time. They may make a statement, perhaps as a response to a specific question; then having made that statement they might need to qualify it. They might then be reminded of something else they wish to add and so on. In this way, a monologue can be regarded as a series of interrelated thoughts. Communicating a character's thought processes is fundamental to any acting technique. In the case of an audition, it takes the pressure off having to deliver a load of text. It allows you to stay fresh, to be in the moment and to make spontaneous choices. Before you start, all you need worry about is the trigger – the reason for saying what you do. Then have the courage to take it thought by thought and allow yourself to be surprised. In this way the monologue should feel slightly different every time.

- It is vital that you use your imagination to envisage all that the character sees and describes. If you are still seeing the page on which the speech is written, you know you are doing something wrong. Provide images for yourself so that in your mind's eye you quite literally lift the speech from the page.

- Timing/editing. Most speeches at audition should last no longer than two minutes. Some of the monologues in this edition are slightly longer, some shorter. Some I have cut, and some I have edited from a duologue with another character, and some have been augmented by joining two or more passages which appear separately in the original text. I have inserted this empty bracket symbol […] to show where a cut has been made. Once you have read the whole play, you may have ideas of your own about what and what not to include.

☞ THE AUDITION

You will find there are many useful books on the market that make a complete study of this subject, from what to wear to how to enter and exit a room. These are some of the basics:

- *Manage your nerves.* Try to put the increased adrenaline you are experiencing to good use. Approach the audition with a positive sense of excitement, something to which you have been looking forward as opposed to something you have been dreading. Nervous energy, if correctly channelled, can help at an audition. Conversely you should avoid being under-energised. If you are someone who reacts lethargically to increased stress, you may need to do a good warm-up before you arrive.

- *Take ownership of the situation.* Before you begin, take a moment to imagine the space you are in as the location of the monologue. The best auditions are those in which the actor successfully transports the panel from, say, 'Studio One or Two' (or whatever the room you are auditioning in is called) to an urban street, a clearing in the woods, a room in a flat in modern Russia, etc. Take time to think about where you will place the other character/s in the scene and, before you speak, allow yourself a moment to hear what has been said to you or to imagine what has just happened that prompts you to say the things you do. Do not rush the speech. Take your time. In the case of a drama-school audition, remember that you will be paying for this privilege!

• *Empower yourself.* There is no good reason why the panel should want you to fail. If you are auditioning for a youth group or a drama school, consider that the panel are willing you to do well, even if they are not necessarily giving that impression. If you have been asked to be seen for a specific role, it is because the director is serious about you for the job. It is possible that the panel are equally anxious about the impression they may give you. Remember, you only have control over your part of the audition process. There is no point speculating, worrying about whether they will want you in their group, school or offer you the part. Just take care of your side of things, and be safe in the knowledge that, whatever happens, you tried your best.

☞ HOW TO USE THIS BOOK

For each monologue, I have provided a list of the following:

☞ WHO   The character's name, their age, and where they come from. As a general rule, it is best to avoid accents unless they are native to you, or you have a good ear for them, or you wish to practise them. If the character's accent is not native to you, you may like to try playing the speech in your own accent, but watch out for speeches that have been written with a strong dialect or idiom. These do not translate well as they disturb the rhythm and overall feeling of the piece.

☞ TO WHOM   It is useful to think of a monologue as an uninterrupted duologue or dialogue. Rather than talking to a blank wall, see if you can visualise the person or people to

whom you are speaking. Cast them in your mind's eye.
Imagine their reactions as you progress with your speech.
How does their response in turn affect you. Are you in love
with them? Do they make you blush? Do you feel negatively
towards them? Can you read their disapproval? Whatever the
relationship, the panel will need to believe that you are
actually talking to somebody. It is advisable, by the way, not to
look directly at the panel, unless they ask you to do so.

Direct audience address: If your character is talking to the
audience, make a decision about who the audience are to you.
Are they your friend and your confidant? Are they more like
an analyst with whom you feel safe to reveal your innermost
thoughts? Are they a sort of sounding board? Are they judging
you? Do you need to explain yourself or to convince them in
some way? It is still advisable not to look at the actual panel in
this case, but imagine an audience just above their heads and
direct your speech there.

☞ WHERE   For the most part, this is specified in the text.
Take a moment before you start your speech to imagine the
location.

☞ WHEN   Most of the monologues in this volume are set in
the present day. Some are historical. Read the play to make
further decisions about the time of year, day of the week and
the time of day it is.

☞ WHAT TO CONSIDER   This will include the style of the
play, its themes and use of language, the character's backstory
and some indication about what happens next.

☞ WHAT HE WANTS   Objectives to play. Once you have
learned your speech, done all the necessary research and
provided images for yourself of all that your character
describes, the only thing you should be actively playing is the
'What do I want?' or the 'What do I have to have?'

☞ KEYWORDS   There are usually one or two keywords in a
sentence that portray the meaning. This does not mean to say
that you should overemphasise these words or use increased
volume, rather be aware that they are often specifically chosen

by the character for a purpose or resonate in a way that may be out of the ordinary. You will probably find that these are the words to which you will need to connect (intellectually and imaginatively) in order to get beneath the skin of your character. In some cases, the writer is so descriptive that you will be able to add more words to the list as it stands.

*

These prompts are a suggestion only. When you become increasingly familiar with your speech, you will find you have opinions of your own; you may even find yourself in disagreement. No two actors are exactly alike just as no two people can be. It is a very personal endeavour. Use this book as a starting point from which you will form your own ideas. It is by no means a substitute for reading the play, but rather a tool intended to help, to provoke and hopefully to inspire.

The Monologues

3 Sisters on Hope Street

Diane Samuels and Tracy Ann-Oberman

☞ **WHO**   Arnold Lasky, thirty-five, Jewish, from Liverpool.

☞ **TO WHOM**   His dead father.

☞ **WHERE**   The living room of the Lasky family house, Hope Street, Liverpool.

☞ **WHEN**   Monday 5th July 1948.

☞ **WHAT HAS JUST HAPPENED**   Arnold Lasky and two of his three sisters have been living in the family home, bequeathed to them on the death of their father a year earlier. Arnold is a talented scholar. He speaks several languages and is a gifted artist and musician, but when he falls in love with local girl, Debbie Pollack, and subsequently marries her, his hopes turn sour. His wife is overbearing and, following the birth of their son, Arnold loses all artistic and academic ambitions. Having been roped into working for the council, he gives up on his PhD. Then, while his wife embarks on an affair with Councillor Peter O'Donnell, Arnold, who is now also working as an accountant for Debbie's father, a butcher, slips further and further into debt. He has a gambling habit, which is costly, and, by the end of the play, having first remortgaged the house without the sisters' permission, he is forced to sell it to his father-in-law. Here, as he is pressured to make over the deeds, he imagines talking to his dead father and wonders what he would have made of it all.

☞ **WHAT TO CONSIDER**

- Gertie, Rita and May are the names of his three sisters.
- As the only boy he was adored and much money was spent on his education.
- He knows he has wasted his time and squandered his opportunities. Worst of all, he has disappointed his sisters. Decide to what extent his gambling is a reaction to his overwhelming sense of failure.
- His sister, May, describes him as having become 'fat and sweaty'.

- By the time of the monologue, Arnold and Debbie have had two children. Arnold has come to loathe his wife.

- Familiarise yourself with the plight of the Jews during the Second World War and the key political and historical events that lead to the formation of Palestine as the new Jewish State.

- 'Kvetch' is a Yiddish word meaning to complain, grumble or moan.

- 'Yom Tov' are Jewish holidays.

- The play is a reworking of Chekhov's *Three Sisters*. You may like to read the original.

☞ **WHAT HE WANTS**

- His father's approval. (Regardless of the fact that it is too late.)

- To give vent to his feelings of frustration and claustrophobia.

- To justify his own weakness at what he is about to do.

- Forgiveness.

☞ **KEYWORDS**   existed   weighty   bought   sell   expect expecting   snuffed   interfering   nowhere

Arnold

❝ Well, Daddy, are you watching this?

He picks up a pen from the table.

When did you and Mummy first take over from the Weinbergs and move in here? Before the Great War. Before the four of us existed. And now you're a grandpa, so I'm sure you'll understand that our Bobby and baby Marilyn must be well taken care of. That's the only reason I'm doing this, Daddy. And Joe Pollack is family. A more doting grandpa you couldn't hope to find. And the mortgage is weighty. I don't suppose that this is quite what you hoped for me. To be bought out. Or to sell out. Depends how you look at it. But then not much ends up how we expect, does it, Daddy, when you're stuck in a

community of, what, ten thousand Jews, that seems like it's
about fifty thousand strong. God help me. Small-minded
busybodies always poking their nose in, giving advice,
expecting you to fit in and not stand out. And all they care
about isn't learning and books and the meaning of life or the
beauty of art, but what they eat and what's scarce and endless
bloody weather and could they one day afford their own car or
even a television, now wouldn't that be something? And they
enjoy a few drinks and cigarettes, if they can get hold of any
these days, and a good gossip and a right old kvetch and bit of
rumpy-pumpy behind the hubby's back and a new hat for Yom
Tov and on and on and on it goes, and this is what they teach
the kids whose spark of life is snuffed out just like theirs so
that they carry on being the same small-minded, tunnel-
visioned, self-important, interfering busybodies going
nowhere for ever!

He looks through the papers sadly.

Oh Gertie. Oh Rita. Dearie, dearie me. Oh May. **99**

55 Days

Howard Brenton

☞ **WHO**   Oliver Cromwell, Lieutenant General, MP and second-in-command of the Parliamentary Army.

☞ **TO WHOM**   Lord Thomas Fairfax, Commander-in-Chief of the Parliamentary Army.

☞ **WHERE**   Cromwell's billet in a room above a tavern, Knottingley, Yorkshire.

☞ **WHEN**   December 1648.

☞ **WHAT HAS JUST HAPPENED**   The play tells the story of the fifty-five days that preceded the execution of King Charles I. The monologue comes close to the start of the play in the first of Cromwell's scenes. So far we know that Parliament has voted against bringing the King to trial and that the Army, angry at the outrage, has taken it upon itself to 'purge' Parliament of those who would seek to protect the King. Chiefly the Presbyterians, to whom the King has promised that he will rid the church of Bishops. Cromwell was in Pontefract at the time, where he has been fighting continued opposition. In this scene, Fairfax himself, Commander-in-Chief of the Parliamentary Army and very much opposed to the purge, has travelled a night and a day to inform Cromwell of the news. He demands to know whether Cromwell supports such a purge and wonders whether it is he who has ordered it. Cromwell tells Fairfax that he did not order the purge, but accepts that the Army has its own mind and for that reason he cannot condemn the purge. The speech follows their heated exchange.

☞ **WHAT TO CONSIDER**

- For six years the country has been ravaged by a bitter Civil War.
- Read the play and familiarise yourself with its historical and political context.
- Both Cromwell and the King are convinced that God is on their side.

☞ WHAT HE WANTS

- An end to the fighting.
- Reassurance from Fairfax.
- A sign or a message from God.

☞ KEYWORDS   skirmish   sneaking   siege   scrap   screeching
safe   surrender   horror   Devil   starved   hatred

Cromwell

❝ Let me tell you what I saw this morning. I was out with a company from the Ferrybridge encampment, what, a mile from Pontefract? There was a skirmish, a group of the King's Scots fighters sneaking away from the siege. We cornered them in a scrap of woodland. I called out, 'Lads, lads, don't fight, no cause. You have no cause.' All but one ran off, dropping their weapons, but that one, he came at us screeching like a devil. A musketeer fired, he went down… […] And I saw… it was a boy. What, thirteen? I knelt down to help the wound, it was not too bad. I asked him where he was from. Lanark, he said. Lanark, the Scottish Lowlands, good farming country. 'What are you fighting for, lad?' I said. 'For good King Charles,' he said. 'And what did King Charles ever give you?' I asked. 'Five shilling,' he said. 'And promise of no bishops.' […] But I thought: this boy, maybe this is the Lord coming to our aid! I said, 'If you're a godly lad, go back to Pontefract, tell your officers they can have safe passage back to Scotland. Surrender and we can all go back to our farms.' 'Who says so?' he asked. 'Lieutenant General Cromwell says so,' I replied. And… and… […] The horror. On his face. The horror. 'The Devil!' he shouted, staring at me. 'The Devil's breath on me! The Devil!' He got to his feet, the musketeer had reloaded. 'No, don't fire,' I said. 'Let him go.' What do you think, Thomas, will the boy see his country again, his family farm? If they're not all starved to death? […] The hatred. What can we do about the hatred? **❞**

About A Goth*

Tom Wells

☞ **WHO**   Nick, seventeen, a goth.

☞ **TO WHOM**   The audience (see note on 'Direct audience address' in the introduction).

☞ **WHERE**   Unspecified. Perhaps Nick's bedroom and then his kitchen, you decide.

☞ **WHEN**   Present day.

☞ **WHAT HAS JUST HAPPENED**   This speech is the start of a much longer monologue that forms a short play.

☞ **WHAT TO CONSIDER**

- The play, narrated by Nick in the present tense, traces the events of a life-changing day. It is intercut with recollections from the past.

- Nick is gay.

- He has feelings for Greg, and later on in the play it seems as though these may be reciprocated.

- Nick's love of the Existentialists. You might like to read Camus' *The Stranger*, if you have not already done so.

- By the end of the day, Nick is no longer a goth.

☞ **WHAT HE WANTS**

- To give vent to his feelings of frustration.

- To separate himself from the herd.

- To provide for himself a strong identity. To what extent does being a goth give him this?

- To find an outlet for his intelligent and highly sensitive nature.

- To figure out, firstly, why Greg has not called, and then, subsequently, what Greg's postcard might signify.

---

* Published in the volume *Me, As A Penguin*

☞ **KEYWORDS** (*there are many*) coffin hate die stains dark tragic/tragedies turmoil burden loneliness foreboding misery

☞ **NB** This play offers a number of other speeches from which to choose.

Nick

❝ As beds go it is passable, I suppose. Obviously I would prefer to sleep in a coffin but as my mum has so hilariously pointed out, they don't sell coffins at IKEA.

Yet.

[…]

I check my phone but. Nothing. Greg still hasn't replied to my text. It has been three days and eleven hours now, which seems a bit relaxed even for someone as simple as him. Look in my sent messages. It's there in capital letters:

I HATE MYSELF AND I WANT TO DIE.

I wonder if I've been too subtle again. Probably. I forget not everyone is as emotionally mature and sensitive as me. I decide to have a wank, but even that is doomed. Halfway through, I start worrying about getting stains on my new black duvet cover. My heart isn't in it after that. […]

Breakfast is depressing as usual. All I want is to read Camus and eat my Coco Pops, but it is so hard to concentrate with Dad's armour clanking and Mum clattering about with her tankards in the sink. […] Honestly. It's tragic. Everyone else's parents lie and cheat and have inner turmoil and chuck teapots at each other. I get the world's most cheerful medieval re-enactors. My mum leans over, dangles her fluted sleeve in my chocolatey milk, passes me a postcard. It's got a donkey on the front. Looking jaunty.

'Camping is amazing.'

Three exclamation marks.

'Weather perfect.'

A further two exclamation marks.

'Dropped my phone off a cliff to prove it is shatterproof. It's not. That was my old phone. Brilliant.'

Underlined.

'Bet your missing me.'

'Your' spelt wrong.

'You big gay.'

No comment.

'Greg.'

And a kiss.

Pause.

'Fancy finishing off this mead?'

Mum holds out a bottle.

I give her a long, stern look.

'Wench, I do not.'

The bus isn't due for another ten minutes so I undo one of my badges and self-harm for a bit. I don't draw blood cos my cloak is dry clean only but it helps pass the time. The bus stop smells of piss and regret. It's a very sunny day, the worst kind of weather for a goth, so I lurk in the shadows contemplating the great tragedies of my life. The burden of my intelligence, for example. Loneliness.

I am an only child.

Unless you count Lizzie, my sister […]

Right on cue, she drives past the bus stop. […]

'Alright, gorgeous,' she says.

I could vom.

'Need a lift into town?' […]

I get dropped off at the mini-roundabout. There is a sense of foreboding and quite a big Starbucks. I buy a Mint Frappuccino, the most gothic of the available drinks, and finish it in the cemetery next door. […] I've got a muffin too but I'm saving it till afterwards. Give me something to live for. Cos looking round me, the graves have never seemed more inviting. In the end, though, it's time. I slurp the last minty dregs and head off for another two hours of misery. **99**

Angels

Ronan O'Donnell

☞ **WHO**   Nick Prentice, thirty-one, security guard, Scottish. He speaks with a strong accent and in local dialect.

☞ **TO WHOM**   The audience (see note on 'Direct audience address' in the introduction).

☞ **WHERE**   A police interview room, Edinburgh.

☞ **WHEN**   Present day.

☞ **WHAT HAS JUST HAPPENED**   This speech forms the start of a one-man play in which security guard, Nick Prentice, is interrogated by a violent policeman following the mysterious death of a petty shoplifter.

☞ **WHAT TO CONSIDER**

- The story is told in the present tense as if it is happening now. Provide for yourself strong visual images of all that you describe.

- The heightened style of the play. The story is surreal. The language poetic.

- Nick is a fantasist. He is obsessed with the actress Scarlett Johansson and has been writing an erotic story about her entitled 'Angels'.

- The use of idiom, e.g: 'wit' = 'what' / 'keekin' = 'peeping' / 'jannie' = 'janitor' / 'snout' = 'tobacco' / 'aw' = 'all' / 'wance' = 'once'.

☞ **WHAT HE WANTS**

- To paint as clear a picture as he can of what he sees, smells and feels. Note the intricate detail with which he describes the scene as if his eyes were a camera going in close.

- To share his dread of the violence that awaits him. To what extent does he regard the audience as an important witness to events?

- To protest his innocence.

☞ **KEYWORDS**   fizzes   fossily   excremental   spurting gurning   gasping   golden   toasty   crinkly   fumbled   grime

☞ **NB**   This play offers a number of other speeches from which to choose.

Nick

❝ Interview room's tiny – way overheated, bit of a jannie's kip hole under the school boiler room – no windows just a long tube o neon leaking its light from behind a security grill. Now an again the neon fizzes – erratically blinks – snap, dork, snap! I adjust my eyes. Here, time crawls backwards into its fossily shell. But I feel grateful for that. Not sure why. Maybe it's like the interval between blows. It's no like anybody has hit me yet, but you would value greatly the interval between blows, wouldn't you? You would value tiny inconsequential routines in a room like this and wrap the grey stretch about you like an auld stale blanket. Check this oot – it's boiling hot but my hands are shaking. I looks about me for the first time. The walls are covered in excremental slogans. Underpass graffiti. A forest o cocks and balls o various sizes with tears of spurting cum. You wonder at the ingenuity since the writings are scratched and gouged and wrote in smoke, an the ceiling too is covered in tags and wit look like Banksy-inspired stencils o venomous monkeys. Gurning baboon faces peering through the swastikas. The room has a smack and smell all o its own – It's like keekin through a loom o smoke although there's a large no-smoking sign on the wall in front o me and I canny imagine the rules being flaunted willy-nilly round here – I'm gasping for a fag. I can smell the golden toasty fumes. Oh, for the crinkly plastic wrapping an the swan-white fag papers an the horsehair snout. The fumbled rolling an ritual o a single-skinner. But for all its uncared-for grime I know I'm in a room o iron protocol. No smoking. It's as if the graffiti is aw that's left wance the shouting an bawling has been drained away. And in regard to this room the graffiti's akin to the red-velvet upholstery o a theatre box at the King's, part o the essential decor o the place. A perfect room to put the boot in. ❞

Apologia

Alexi Kaye Campbell

☞ **WHO**   Simon, strictly speaking thirties, but because he is talking about an event in the past, he could be played younger.

☞ **TO WHOM**   Kristin, his mother.

☞ **WHERE**   The kitchen of Kristin's converted farmhouse, somewhere in the English countryside.

☞ **WHEN**   Present day. The middle of the night.

☞ **WHAT HAS JUST HAPPENED**   Kristin is a celebrated art historian. She holds strong feminist and left-wing views. Throughout her adult life she has been a staunch campaigner and political activist. She has recently published an autobiography but without once mentioning that she has two sons. When Peter, her eldest, and then Simon, her youngest, arrive to celebrate her birthday, the now grown-up sons confront their mother about the way in which she has neglected them. The speech that follows is made up of Simon's share of his conversation with Kristin.

☞ **WHAT TO CONSIDER**

- Simon is having a nervous breakdown.
- He says he feels 'disjointed', 'dislocated', 'disillusioned', 'disturbed', 'distracted' and 'discombobulated'.
- The week before, he disappeared for three days and was living rough.
- He has had three jobs in as many months.
- He considers himself a writer and has an unfinished novel. He has been working on it for seven years.
- He has a girlfriend called Claire, an actress in a popular television series. Claire has been cheating on him.
- Before he arrived tonight he cut his hand on broken glass. Kristin has been cleaning his wound.

- After their parents' divorce (when Simon was seven), Simon and his brother were brought up by their father. Simon felt abandoned. Read the play to understand fully the complexity of Simon's relationship with his mother.

☞ WHAT HE WANTS

- To give vent to his feelings of hurt and resentment.
- To shame his mother. (Note how he too felt shame.)
- To pinpoint the events in his life that go some way to explaining why he feels 'disjointed'.
- To understand why it is that he cannot cope.
- To feel safe. Note the significance of Kristin tending to his hand as if he were a little boy.

☞ KEYWORDS   dark   wrong   nervous   shaking   weak broken   staring   jammed   strange   foreign

Simon

66 Do you remember once I came to Italy on my own? It was the summer. I must have been – what – eleven? […] Dad put me on the train in London. You were supposed to pick me up in Genoa. […] But something happened and you never made it. I mean, you did eventually but it was like a day later. […] I remember all the trains had come in and all the people had been greeted by their families or friends and I sat watching them and waiting to spot your face in the crowd. […] But it got dark and you never came. […] It must have been one in the morning and I was lying on this bench when this man approached me. […] He asked me if I was all right – […] And I said that I was and that I was waiting for my mother but that she would be there soon and that I would wait for her until she got there. […] And then he said, 'Why don't you come back to my house and have something to eat and you can rest and then I'll bring you back in the morning.' […] And even though […] I *knew* […] that it was wrong for me to follow this

man back to his house, I stood up and picked up my bag and followed him. […] And part of me was thinking – 'This will show her, this will show her, this will fucking show her.' […] So we walked through the streets of Genoa and […] eventually we got to this old building. […] His flat was at the top and he opened the door and let me in. He asked me to sit down and then he gave me a glass of wine and made some joke about not telling my parents. […] And then he cooked a meal. […] He made pasta with a tomato sauce […] and I noticed that he was nervous and that his hands were shaking a little and I could feel the wine whooshing around in my head. […] I asked him if I could use the bathroom so he took me down the hall and showed me where it was. […] I remember the light in the bathroom was very weak as if the bulb was broken or something, it was quite dark. So that when I looked into the mirror I could only just see my face. I stood there for some time just staring at myself and wondering why you hadn't shown up at the station. […] And it was when I was trying to see my face in the mirror that I heard him breathing outside the door. So he'd been standing there all along, on the other side of the door. And then I tried to open it, to open the door but it was jammed. […] As if he was blocking it from the other side. […] Then after a little it opened and he wasn't there. He was back in the kitchen. So I went back. […] After we'd eaten […] he asked me if I wanted to sleep in his bed with him and I said that I didn't. Then he took some sheets out of a cupboard and turned the sofa into a bed for me and then he said he'd wake me at six in the morning and walk me back to the station. And that's what he did. […] Lately I can't seem to get that night out of my head. I keep thinking of myself trying to find my face in the mirror in the dim-lit bathroom of that dark building in that strange and foreign city. […] Where were you? […] Where were you? Where were you? […] You were never there. **99**

Before It Rains

Katherine Chandler

☞ **WHO**   Carl, a violent and volatile young man, Welsh.

☞ **TO WHOM**   Michael, his 'friend'.

☞ **WHERE**   The woods on the edge of a council estate in Cardiff.

☞ **WHEN**   Present day, a Sunday, early evening.

☞ **WHAT HAS JUST HAPPENED**   Set on a run-down council estate in Cardiff, the play tells the story of Michael, who suffers from Asperger's syndrome, and his single-parent mother Gloria, who struggles to cope. When Carl and his family arrive on the estate they set about intimidating fellow residents. Carl is almost feral. His elder brother is violent and their father sadistic. Carl befriends Michael and encourages him in antisocial behaviour. Carl and his brother enjoy setting rat traps in the woods. But when they turn their attentions to killing people's pets, the police are called out. Their father's response is to beat them. Here in the play, Carl has run away from home and is hiding in the woods following a particularly vicious attack by the father on Carl's brother, 'our Kid'.

☞ **WHAT TO CONSIDER**

- Carl is both violent and vulnerable.

- He saw a documentary about a Russian boy who was brought up by wolves in the wild. He strongly identifies with him.

- His mother left when he was a child.

- He has grown up with the idea that a man should live in a pack with other men: 'No pussy bitches giving me all that.'

- The betrayal he feels at the hand of his father.

- His relationship with Michael and Gloria. Read the play to understand fully its complexity.

☞ WHAT HE WANTS

- To protect and to be protected.
- To escape the brutal dominance of his father.
- A sense of belonging.
- Michael's help.

☞ KEYWORDS   blood   blade   sliced   wolves   cub   sinking
skin   veins   heart   trust

Carl

❝ I can't get the fucking blood off, it's over my hands and my gear and I can't get it off. Our kid, he's sat there and I'm trying to hold his face together and there's fucking blood everywhere, man. And my old man just keeps at him. And I'm telling him to fucking leave him alone.

It'll be me next time.

And he'll come at me worse just to teach me. He's gone at him with this blade, see, sliced his face. And I can see his teeth, through his cheek. And I'm trying to hold his face.

I'm holding our kid's face together and in my head I'm thinking about the wolves. About the wolves and the Russian. About how they looks after each other. Looks out for each other.

An' I looks at my ol' man an' he won't call for the fucking ambulance in case he gets himself banged up again. He's calling us pussy shits an' kicking off. His cub is fucking bleeding half his face off an' he won't do fuck all.

I'm looking at this blood. On my hands. Sinking in my skin. An' in this blood I'm seeing our kid an' I'm seeing my ol' man. An' I'm seeing me. I'm in there too, Mikey. An' then I'm seeing that it's in me, that blood. That it's running through me an' there's no escaping it, Mikey. I can see it. There's no fucking escaping it cos it's through my veins an' it's beating through my heart an' it's him.

He's in me.

Whatever I do, Mikey. […]

I got nowhere to go, Mikey. An' if anything's happened to our kid. I don't know, Mikey. I don't know what happened. Is he dead, Mikey? I ran.

I got no one.

'Cept you.

I can trust you, can't I, Mikey? […]

Cos if I'm gonna make it out here I gotta be able to trust you. **"**

Boys

Ella Hickson

☞ **WHO**   Cam, twenty-one, Scottish.

☞ **TO WHOM**   His flatmates, Benny, Mack and Timp, Timp's
girlfriend Laura and Mack's secret lover Sophie.

☞ **WHERE**   The kitchen of a five-room student flat in
Edinburgh.

☞ **WHEN**   Present day, summer.

☞ **WHAT HAS JUST HAPPENED**   It is the end of term and the
contract is up on the flat Cam shares with Benny, Mack and Timp.
The boys have been partying and when the play opens it is the
morning after the night before. Cam, who has crashed out under
the kitchen table, wakes up woozily. He is a virtuoso violinist and
is nervous about an extremely important concert he will be
playing at later that night. It could make or break his career. He
confesses to Benny that he is terrified and that a large part of
him does not want to perform. He feels as though a career as a
concert violinist has not been his choice and that he cannot
stand the pressure. Benny calms him down and convinces him
that rather than dropping out he should at least go and try to do
his best. Cam is grateful to Benny for the good advice. Then,
while Cam is away at the concert, the others enjoy another night
of partying. When Cam arrives back, triumphant, they are drunk
and high. They ask him how it went.

☞ WHAT TO CONSIDER

- When he was ten years old, Cam's mother inadvertently lied
  about his age. The deception continued. He now says he is
  nineteen, when in fact he is twenty-one.

- In the competitive world of serious music, this two-year
  difference ensures that Cam retains his 'prodigy' status. To
  what extent does this feed Cam's feeling that the whole
  'virtuoso violinist' thing is a sham, not of his choosing and that
  he wants out?

- In a dark twist to the story, this is strangely resolved. Read the play to find out what happens next.

- It is an unusually hot summer, and a local strike means the dustbins have not been cleared. The smell of rotting rubbish pervades the scenes.

- While the boys are playing inside, fuelled by a cocktail of drugs and alcohol, outside there is growing civil disobedience and a riot ensues.

☞ WHAT HE WANTS

- To bask in his moment of glory.
- To share his success with his friends.
- To rest in a moment of clarity, when all the hard work, stress and uncertainty feel as though they have been worth it. You may like to draw on your own experiences of acting, the fear and triumph of putting on a play, to connect to this fully.

☞ KEYWORDS   intense   amazing   nervous   glint   noise clapping   mad   moisture   silent   hovering   creak   great

☞ NB   This play offers a number of other speeches from which to choose.

Cam

  " God – it's nice to be back here. It was fucking intense. […] It was – pretty amazing. I've never – I was really fucking nervous but… I don't think I've ever seen that many people – I mean except for football matches, but… […] I was so fucking nervous, I kept having to dry my hands, I swear I was actually sweating through my fingertips and I was so worried I was going to… but you know waiting to walk out there and you can just about see all those people and the lights are real bright and – fuck, my heart's still beating like the fucking – and you stand there and you see the glint on glasses and the odd grin but not much else so you're not really sure that they're there and – they start clapping and man – that many people – and the noise, the noise was so loud it made the stage shake a little bit, I felt it through my feet, the clapping, it was mad. And all the moisture goes out your mouth and suddenly you're standing in front of them and it's dead dead silent and – that was sort of the best bit – just when I was about to play and my bow is just a wee way off the strings – just waiting there – hovering – and it's there and you're still and then you hear this little tiny noise, this little fucking seat creak and you realise that fucking hundreds of people just leant in – just a fraction – to hear what you're going to do next – waiting for you to start. […] I did my thing. […] big old hoo-ha after. Everyone fucking talking to me and offering me shit and that guy – the Russian – […] He wants to teach me – one on one – in fucking Vienna – I don't even know where that is! […] They all stood and clapped and – it was – it was – great. It was really really great. (*Pause*.) You guys are totally fucked. […] Let's fucking party! **"**

Bully Boy

Sandi Toksvig

☞ **WHO**   Eddie, twenty, a soldier from Burnley.

☞ **TO WHOM**   Major Oscar Hadley.

☞ **WHERE**   A military aeroplane en route from Iraq to the UK.

☞ **WHEN**   Present day.

☞ **WHAT HAS JUST HAPPENED**   Major Oscar Hadley has been sent to Iraq to investigate the alleged misconduct of the 'Bully Boy' unit and in particular Eddie Clark, a young squaddie from Burnley who has been accused of the murder of an eight-year-old-Iraqi boy. During the investigation, Eddie has been kept apart from the other members of the team, all witnesses to the crime. On a journey back to base from the village they patrol, Eddie and the Major are in a separate truck from the others. There is an ambush. Eddie saves the Major, who has been knocked unconscious by the blast, but when he goes to check on the other vehicle he finds his friends have perished. Here, on a flight back to England, waking from a nightmare, Eddie recalls what happened.

☞ **WHAT TO CONSIDER**

- Eddie joined the army at sixteen. He says there was 'Nothing else to do'.

- Major Oscar Hadley had already been injured in the Falklands and is in a wheelchair.

- The play explores not only the physical trauma but also the harrowing psychological effect of war.

- To what extent does Eddie feel a survivor's guilt and a helplessness for not having been able to save his friends?

- Read the play to see how the relationship between Oscar and Eddie develops, and how Eddie struggles to cope with life back home.

☞ WHAT HE WANTS

- To punish Oscar. Note how he blames Oscar for the fact that he was separated from his friends.

- To torture himself for not having been there.

- To forgive his friends for having betrayed him. (It is not until later in the play that we discover Oscar has lied to him and that, in fact, nothing had been said to incriminate Eddie.)

☞ KEYWORDS determined white angry shock hot liquid exploding drenched poured smell empty box/boxes

Eddie

❝ I can't stop thinking about it. You don't remember, do you? Wish I'd had a blow to the head. […] You were so determined I wouldn't speak to the lads. I should have been with them. You made me go with you in the vehicle in front. We were moving so slow. Just been through the checkpoint. I'd been sitting next to you. The convoy got held up. I don't know what. Goats. Fucking goats or something. You let me get out. Check ahead. […] People talk about explosions but you don't know, do you? Not really? Everything went white. Knocked the shit out of me. Improvised Explosive Device, my arse. They're getting better and better. Vehicle landed on its side and you were out cold. I knew you couldn't get out even if you woke. You were taking us back to base. The others were in the vehicle behind. Brian, Jack, Paki, Harley. My mates. The Bully Boys. I thought they were my mates but you said they told you about the boy. Said I killed him. After all we'd been through. I was angry with them. I don't want to be angry with them… not now…

The blast took half the road with it. Funny thing is, their vehicle looked fine. Honestly. Just the same as before. I ran to the back to open up. Get them out. I thought they were alright because there was no noise. I couldn't hear any noise from inside but you know, shock, maybe they were shocked. I couldn't get the doors open. I was pulling at them. The handle was hot. Then the doors burst open. It was the liquid, you see. Like a fire hose of hot liquid exploding over me. There was nothing but liquid. Just liquid. Hot liquid where the lads had been and it drenched me. My friends poured over me. The smell.

[…]

I can't stop thinking about them. In the back of the plane except not really. Not really there. Just an empty box. Boxes. Four boxes. **99**

Chatroom[*]

Enda Walsh

☞ **WHO**   Jim, fifteen.

☞ **TO WHOM**   Eva, fifteen.

☞ **WHERE**   The conversation takes place in an internet chatroom, but we assume that Jim is in his bedroom.

☞ **WHEN**   Present day.

☞ **WHAT HAS JUST HAPPENED**   The play follows the conversations of six teenagers who meet and chat online. William and Jack have been discussing the merits of children's literature, Emily and Eva, the pernicious influence of Britney Spears, Laura has been listening to Jim, who is depressed. Then William, Jack, Emily and Eva come together to form a chatroom they call 'Chiswick's Bloody Opinionated'. Jim joins the group late one night. He wants to talk about his depression. Emily is sympathetic to Jim, but when she tells the group about her own experience of anorexia, the others ridicule her, and she leaves the chatroom. William then asks for a private chat with Jack, leaving Jim alone with Eva. William is bored and is looking for 'a cause'. As we are about to learn in the following scene, William's plan is to toy with Jim, to 'Mess him up a bit. See how far he'll go'. He wants to encourage Jim to kill himself publicly as an act of solidarity with all forgotten teenagers. Eva is already having the same idea, and now that she is alone with Jim she plans to get him to talk. Jim's speech comes in response to Eva's: 'So tell me about the day your father went missing.'

☞ **WHAT TO CONSIDER**

- Jim has been talking to Laura in a suicide chatroom. Is he really ill or does he just need someone with whom to talk?

- Jim is one of four brothers growing up in a single-parent family. Decide to what extent this has fed his need for attention.

* Published in the volume *Enda Walsh Plays: One*

- Jim seems to hold himself responsible for the fact that his father walked out. The point of the day Jim describes was for father and son to bond. This clearly did not happen. Decide to what extent Jim blames himself for his father's disappearance.

- The significance of Jim at first being very fat and then not eating, the stress it placed on his father and then the relief when he started to eat again. Decide to what extent this is somehow linked to the milk and biscuits that Jim gets for himself at the end of that day, and the overall need to please his father.

☞ WHAT HE WANTS

- To be heard and to be understood.
- To be forgiven.
- Reassurance that he was and is not a bad boy.

☞ KEYWORDS   bond   worried   alone   worry   stay

Jim

❝ Right, well, I'm six years old and my three brothers are going away with my mother for the weekend… a treat for something or other. My dad's staying behind and my mother says that he's to look after me. That it would be a chance for us to bond. So they're gone and me and my dad are sat at the kitchen table looking at each other. Like we're looking at each other for the first time, you know. He asks me what I want to do and straight away I say I want to go and see the penguins in the zoo. When I was six I was going through some mad penguin obsession. I used to dress up as a penguin at dinner times and always ask for fish fingers… stuff like that. If it wasn't penguins it was cowboys. Cowboys were cool. A penguin costumed as a cowboy was always a step too far, funnily enough. (*Laughs a little.*) […] So we go to the zoo and I wear my cowboy outfit… get my gun and holster, my hat and all that. We get the bus and it's sort of funny to see my dad on a bus and away from the house. We start to have this chat about when I was born and what a really fat baby I was… but how after a week or so I stopped eating any food and everyone was very worried. That he was very worried. That he was so happy when I got better and they could take me home. (*Slight pause.*) We're in the zoo and I go straight to the penguins. Standing in my cowboy gear… looking at the penguins… having such a great chat to my dad on the bus… it was a perfect childhood day. (*Pause.*) He lets go of my hand and says he'll be back with my choc ice. And he goes. (*Pause.*) He's gone. (*Pause.*) I'm happy looking at the penguins but it's an hour since he's left and I go to look for him. I'm walking about the zoo and I'm not worried yet. And I don't talk to anyone. I leave the zoo and I go to the bus stop we got off at earlier. I get on the bus. I tell the driver my address. He asks where my parents are and I say they're at home waiting for me. I stay on the bus in the seat nearest the driver. After a while we end up at the end of our street and the driver says, 'So long, cowboy.' (*Smiles a little.*) He was nice. (*Pause.*) I get the key from under the mat and open the door and go inside the house. And I'm alone there. I take off my cowboy clothes and hang up my hat and holster. It being Saturday night I have a bath and get into my pyjamas because my dad would have liked that. I have a glass of milk and some biscuits and watch *Stars in Their Eyes* 'cause that was his favourite programme on the telly. (*Slight pause.*) It's getting dark outside and I start to worry. The house is feeling too big so I get my quilt and take it into the bathroom and lock the bathroom door and it feels safer with the door locked so I stay in there. And he's not coming back. (*Pause.*) He's never coming back. (*Pause.*) I stay there for two days. **"**

Cressida

Nicholas Wright

☞ **WHO**   Honey, an eighteen-year-old boy actor.

☞ **TO WHOM**   Stephen, a fourteen-year-old 'would-be' boy actor.

☞ **WHERE**   The costume store of Gunnell's theatre, London.

☞ **WHEN**   1630s

☞ **WHAT HAS JUST HAPPENED**   The play is based on real-life characters who formed part of London's theatre community in the 1630s. Shank is an older actor and trainer of boy players, of whom Honey is the lead. He has two others in his employment. However, in order to stage *A Midsummer Night's Dream*, he needs five more to play the fairies. These he has hired from a rival producer, Master Gunnell. But when one of Gunnell's boys, Stephen Hammerton, arrives at the Globe Theatre with news of Master Gunnell's sudden disappearance, Shank fears he will be ruined. Gunnell has fled to avoid his creditors. Shank had invested five hundred pounds in Gunnell's theatre, with a view to signing up the best boys once Gunnell had trained them. He borrowed the money from the Board of his own theatre and now has to find some way of paying it back. Stephen, who is desperate to be one of Shank's players, asks Honey if he will help him steal costumes from Gunnell's store. In this way he hopes to help raise funds for Shank and in return hopes that Shank will reward him with a place in the company. Stephen, who is in awe of Honey, wants to know what it is that makes him such a good actor. The speech that follows is Honey's response

☞ **WHAT TO CONSIDER**

- The historical background. You may need to familiarise yourself with early-seventeenth-century theatre practice and to read Nicholas Wright's Afterword at the back of the playtext.

- Honey is a well-respected and admired player. Titania is one of his finest roles.

- He is worldly-wise, savvy and a bit of a tart.

- He is on the cusp of manhood and knows that his career is in the balance. By the end of the play he is cast as the Messenger, his hair is short and he has grown a moustache.

- The 'Jhon' to whom he refers is the boys' dresser.

- Honey is high from smoking opium. I do not suggest that you play 'stoned', but you can decide to what extent Honey's vivid description is born out of this altered state.

☞ WHAT HE WANTS

- To reflect on his own success as if he knows it is coming to a close.

- To savour his moment of glory and to rest in its glow.

- To intrigue and to impress Stephen. Honey knows Stephen to be a terrible actor, but nevertheless a potential rival. Decide to what extent Honey is toying with him.

- To explain his sexuality.

☞ KEYWORDS   amazing   flying   wings   stolen   special

Honey

❝ It's different at different times. […] Well, when you're young, you're just a child being clever. Then it changes. […] When you get older. When other boys get tall and clumsy. And their voices drop two million pegs. We don't do that. We hang on. […] We just do. It's like a baby falling down a well. You've got its foot in your hand and you don't let go. So you're not one thing exactly. You're half-man, half-boy. That's when you find you can really do it. And it's amazing. It's better than beer or wine. It's better than smoking. It's like flying. It's like finding that wings have suddenly sprouted from your shoulders. You come on stage and everything happens the way it's meant to. And nobody in the audience looks at anyone else. Because you live in a sort of stolen time that they can't get to. Except through you. And it could disappear at any moment. You're like a soldier on the eve of battle. Every night could be your last. And everyone wants to be that special person on that special night. That's my theory. That's why they grab old Jhon, J, H, O, N, and give him notes for us. It's why they hang about at the Actors' Door.

He puts out the pipe, starts getting out of his dress.

I still get letters every day. Not just from men. Everyone thinks I'm just a boyish bugger. That's not true. I see women as well. They're even stranger than the men are. They ask me to supper and want me to bring my gown and make-up.

He stands, the gown in his arms.

Take it.

We'll carry them back to Shanky. He'll pay his debt to the Board and you'll stay on. Isn't that what you wanted? **99**

Days of Wine and Roses
Owen McCafferty, after JP Miller

☞ **WHO**   Donal, mid-twenties, from Belfast.

☞ **TO WHOM**   Members of an Alcoholics Anonymous meeting.

☞ **WHERE**   London.

☞ **WHEN**   1968.

☞ **WHAT HAS JUST HAPPENED**   The play tells the story of Donal and Mona, both in their twenties, both fleeing Belfast in order to taste life as it is lived in 1960s London. They meet at the airport, subsequently marry and have a son. Donal works for a successful bookmaker, and as the money flows their life becomes one long round of partying. But their 'days of wine and roses' are numbered as they fight to control their alcohol addiction. In the speech that follows, Donal, having arrived at an AA meeting, attempts to confront his demons.

☞ **WHAT TO CONSIDER**

- The play is a reworking of a film script by JP Miller set in Manhattan. You may like to watch the film starring Jack Lemmon and Lee Remick.

- Donal is determined to kick his habit. Mona is in denial about the extent of her addiction. You might like to imagine Mona as someone with whom you are in love or to whom you are very close. In this way you will realise the extent to which Donal must be cruel in order to be kind.

- The shame he feels at his own behaviour.

- The courage it has taken Donal to attend the meeting.

- The language and punctuation. Note how the playwright uses only lower-case letters. There are no commas or full stops, only dashes where a character might take a breath and have a change of thought. What does this suggest to you? How might this determine the playing of the speech in terms of rhythm and pace?

☞ WHAT HE WANTS

- To own up to his addiction.
- To apologise for his wrongdoing and to redress those wrongs.
- To find an answer to why he is the way he is.
- To change.

☞ KEYWORDS   alcoholic   judged   easier   need   good
effort   self-discipline   dignity   saddest   frightens   worse
journey   struggle

Donal

❝ my name is donal mackin and – and i am an alcoholic – the
problem with talking like this – i know that you have all done
this – and that i won't be judged – i had a feeling that would
make this easier – but it isn't – maybe that's it – maybe you
need to do it and then it will be easier – it's just – i don't want
to say things i don't want to say – yet i know deep down those
are the things i need to say – need to get out into the open –
there are other people involved – and i don't know how fair it is
to mention them when they are not here – i have a wife and a
son – i feel like i have taken them on this journey – i feel like i
am a good man – yet i don't act like a good man – i don't put
enough effort into the right type of living to make me a good
man – that's what good people do – they put effort into a
normal type of living – i think that's what they do – i don't
know – maybe i don't even know any good people – i thought
so much about myself i haven't noticed who's been around me
– i'm sorry i know i don't seem to be making any sense – i – my
wife is an alcoholic as well – she doesn't see it like that – but
she is – she thinks all this is just a matter of self-discipline and
dignity – she didn't want me to come here – i can understand
why i didn't want to come myself – she shouted at me before i
left the house this evening – i feel like i've let her down in some
way – not in some way – i have let her down – i have let both of
them down in different ways – her because i'm doing this on

my own – and him because i haven't taken proper notice of him – like all children he's been telling me about his world – and i haven't been listening to him – that's the thing i feel saddest about – it's also the thing that frightens me most – that i have put him second – put everything way down the list – except for drink of course – i don't really want to talk about my wife and child – i've said enough about that – this has to be about me – i know that – that's why i'm here – although in saying that i don't really know how i got here – i do – it's because i had nowhere else to go – i mean i don't know how i got to this point – it feels like it has all just passed me by or something – one minute i've arrived in london to start a new life and the next it's over six years on and i'm explaining myself at an a a meeting – everything was good – it couldn't have been better – married to the woman i love – a beautiful child – and a good job – a job that i liked doing – i had a future – it was as if the drinking caught up with me – i was drinking to be sociable – that's what i thought – it was always part and parcel of what i did – i am – was – a bookie – we were having a ball – people – drink – activity – there was always activity – i always thought that was a good thing – doesn't seem like that now – i sometimes ask myself was it because i was in london – because i was away from home – i'm from belfast – would it have been the same if i had've stayed in belfast – that's not something you can answer is it – something changed in me – i can see that now – i don't really know how to explain this – but it's like life being good isn't really enough – it's as if you go out of your way to make things more difficult for yourself – what you think you're doing is making the world a better place – what you're really doing is the opposite of that – the strange thing is i knew i was doing it – i knew i was making things worse – you can't help yourself – it's not just drink – it's about understanding yourself or something – i don't know – i haven't worked that out yet – maybe that's something you never work out – maybe the journey or the struggle or whatever it is is a lifelong thing – i don't know what's going to happen to me – i just know something has to happen **99**

Delirium

Enda Walsh

☞ **WHO**   Mitya, twenty-seven.

☞ **TO WHOM**   Alyosha, twenty-three, Mitya's brother.

☞ **WHERE**   A room in a Travelodge.

☞ **WHEN**   Present day.

☞ **WHAT HAS JUST HAPPENED**   *Delirium* is based on *The Brothers Karamazov* by Dostoyevsky. It follows the story of three brothers, Mitya, Ivan and Alyosha, their dissolute father Fyodor and their servant Smerdyakov. Mitya is engaged to be married to Katerina, but is in love with his father's whore, Grushenka. Here, Mitya, who has just returned from a holiday in Benidorm, confesses to Alyosha that it is Grushenka, not Katerina, that he loves. He needs to find three thousand pounds in order to pay Katerina back and break off their engagement.

☞ **WHAT TO CONSIDER**

- The heightened realism. The style of the play could be described as Expressionistic. You can therefore be bold in your playing.

- The play's theatricality. Its use of multimedia, dance, song and puppetry.

- Mitya is described by his father as 'a pumped-up ladies' man with more cock than conscience'.

- Alyosha is the only decent person in the play and represents its moral conscience.

- The significance of 'the Karamazov insect'.

☞ **WHAT HE WANTS**

- To make confession.

- For Alyosha to forgive him.

- For Alyosha to help him find the money.

☞ KEYWORDS   (*there are many*) Technicolor   magnificent
dirty   shite   vice   indignity   groping   chafing   grinding
buzzing   glowed   scooped   ashamed

Mitya

❝ Where's the mini-bar?! I need a little confidence for what
I'm about to tell you. You have no idea what it's like living
with this brain. It's like I've been wired by a blind, evil man
who's cracked my skull open and thrown a food mixer
inside… with a fox! A normal person would see a pattern to
the day. Like a series of tasks and challenges that have to be
undertaken, that must be completed. But for me the world
lives in Technicolor, it's a Disneyland with the rides replaced
by pure emotions. Can you imagine such a place? It's
magnificent! And it's SO fucking expensive! I need that three
thousand! Can I speak honestly to you? Will you look past the
drink? (*Slight pause.*) I really would like to be good. (*Slight
pause.*) So this is it, this is why I've called you here, this is the
first part of my confession. […] I love dirty women. I've had a
lot of ladies, of course, but I'm always drawn to the back alleys
behind the main road, to the precious gems in the shite. I'm
speaking figuratively to protect you from the details. But I love
vice. I love the indignity of vice. Besides the indignity of vice
there are other things I love about the world of vice of which
I'm trying very, very, very hard not to speak about to protect
your innocence. The things I'm trying very hard not to speak
about are the firm naked backsides in the alleyways. The pert
nipples that accompany these backsides. The groping… The
exchange of bodily fluids… The chafing… The dull
grinding… The slap-happy sound of skin against skin. Oh
Jesus! Jesus Christ!! (*He adjusts his penis.*) So this is my world,
and into this world stepped Katerina. Back then I was a
lieutenant in the army. I looked great in the uniform. My
colonel, who hated me, had a daughter, Katerina. She was
smart, elegant. Cultured people buzzed about her like
buzzing, cultured things. Everything she touched glowed. The

way that she could turn a phrase. Beautiful details! Once I tried to speak to her, but she looked right through me, Alyosha. I didn't like that. Not long after I discovered that her father owed a lot of money and if he didn't pay it back his family would be fucked. All of a sudden I saw a way to get my own back. I wrote to her. 'If you need the money, come to me in secret; I'm sure we can work something out.' **99**

Eight
Ella Hickson

☞ **WHO**   Jude, eighteen, from an affluent middle-class background.

☞ **TO WHOM**   The audience (see note on 'Direct audience address' in the introduction).

☞ **WHERE**   'A large black block, centre-stage, acts as a bed and a dinner table' – South of France.

☞ **WHEN**   Present day, recounting the events of a year ago.

☞ **WHAT HAS JUST HAPPENED**   This is the start of a longer monologue in which Jude recounts his trip to France and the liaison he has there with an older woman.

☞ **WHAT TO CONSIDER**

- This is one of eight monologues that together form a full-length play.

- As with the other characters in the series, Jude has grown up in a culture that is primarily materialistic. As Ella Hickson writes in her introduction to the play, 'a world in which the central value system is based on an ethic of commercial, aesthetic and sexual excess.'

- Decide to what extent this key experience at seventeen has shaped him.

- Jude's use of language. The speech is highly descriptive, florid even. To what extent is Jude consciously trying to emulate Fitzgerald and Hemingway as he recounts his experience?

☞ **WHAT HE WANTS**

- To distance himself from his father.
- To gain some independence.
- To prove his manhood.

☞ **KEYWORDS**   smacked   burned   strained   squeaked   cracking   reckless   abandon   crazy   crooked   scowling

slammed   crusty   creaked   bikinis   sharp   fluent
looove/lovin

☞ **NB**   This play offers a number of other speeches from
which to choose.

Jude

❝ This time last summer, Dad sent me to the South of
France. The day I left, he stood on the front step and saluted
my departure, like some bloody sergeant-major, pair of baggy
corduroys, copy of the *Guardian* wedged under his arm.

'Off you go, my son,' he yelled. 'You will walk away a boy and
return a man!'

Except I could barely hear him cos he had Haydn's 'Farewell'
Symphony booming out of every window. [...] When I
stepped off the plane, the first thing I felt was the heat – it
smacked me in the face, the stairs burned my feet through my
shoes; I strained to see the city in the distance, but I couldn't
see a thing, I was shitting myself.

Taxi dropped me off at Boulevard Victor Hugo. Now, my dad
would have been in his element. I could hear his voice in my
head: 'Did you know, Jude, that without Victor Hugo, I
strongly doubt we would've ever had Dickens.' Really, Dad,
that's fascinating. I felt for the sandwiches he'd put in the
bottom of my bag, but I'd eaten them on the plane. [...]

Twenty-three, twenty-four – fuck a duck... It was huge.
Wrought-iron gates squeaked open, I carried my suitcase up
to this big green door; the paint was all cracking off it in the
heat. There were old-fashioned shutters and yellow walls. It
looked like all the Riviera photos that Dad had showed me
before I left, all those stories about – (*Sits, imitates Dad,
talking down to imaginary Jude.*) 'Fitzgerald, Picasso and
Hemingway, when genius was valued, Jude, and the women,
oh, the women, beautiful muses with wild eyes and...' Oh,
what did he say?... Oh yeah, 'reckless abandon', as if he was a
hundred years old and he had been there himself – sad act.

I breathed in. I knocked. I was shown to my room by a crazy and crooked-looking woman with fag breath who kept scowling as my bag slammed against the stairs; '*Pardon*,' I whispered weakly, with this pathetic smile like I'd just peed myself. (*Smiles.*) She growled – (*In a growly French accent.*) 'Madame Clara will return later, little boy, for the dinner,' alright. [...] As much as I wanted to be back in Poynton, my French room was... pretty fucking cool. The walls were covered in black-and-white photos that looked like scenes from old movies and that. There was a hat stand, here, in the corner – (*Imitates popping his hat up onto it.*) next to the bookshelf... busting with crusty old novels, all in French, then my window... floor to ceiling, old shutters that proper creaked and a balcony, little radio, huge old mirror – it was brilliant. [...]

Three months here might not be so bad, there was sun and sea and there were bound to be women – (*He thinks.*) in bikinis. I was an independent man, my own room – I could be a Riviera gent; look sharp, become fluent... in the language of looove... eat well, get to know the place, maybe make friends with a... baker. [...]

'Bonjour, Jude!'

'Bonjour, Pierre!'

'Say, Jude, where is that young lady I saw you with, eeh, she is very good-looking, no?

'Eh, Pierre, she some needs some rest... from all the lovin'.' **"**

First Person Shooter

Paul Jenkins

☞ **WHO**   Nugget, a soldier, now in charge of recruitment, fifty (but could be played younger).

☞ **TO WHOM**   Ade, seventeen, a wannabe soldier.

☞ **WHERE**   Army Careers office, Worcester.

☞ **WHEN**   Present day.

☞ **WHAT HAS JUST HAPPENED**   The play tells the story of teenager Ade, his mother Maggie and her colleague Tom. Tom is developing a new technology that will detect faulty rail track ensuring a safer transport system. Maggie is trying to convince him to sell the idea to the Ministry of Defence, who can use the innovation for surveillance operations. Ade, meanwhile, is obsessed with playing violent war games on his games console. He is desperate to try out the simulators the Army use when recruiting and pays a visit to the Army Careers office. Here he meets Nugget, who, understanding that Ade has a completely warped sense of the reality of war, does his very best to dissuade Ade from joining the Army. But Ade has a romantic notion that he has 'to risk my life to take another's.' In the speech that follows, Nugget explains to Ade that war is not necessarily like that and that he himself never did what he was trained to do – actually kill anyone.

☞ **WHAT TO CONSIDER**

• In the context of the play, Nugget is about fifty, if not older. However, out of context and because he is talking about an event in the past, he could be played much younger. If the speech appeals to you why not use the opportunity to create a somewhat different characterisation and backstory for yourself from that of the actual play – one that will fit with your own age. Decide to whom it is you are speaking and why. If you choose to perform this monologue at an audition, make sure you are clear about this to the audition panel if questioned.

- Make a decision about the war to which you refer. Is Nugget talking about the first Gulf War of the early 1990s? How might the speech work if it is used to describe other more recent conflicts?

- Research the time span of the SA80. If you want to contemporise the speech, to what type of gun or rifle might you refer instead? Or just substitute the word 'weapon'.

☞ WHAT HE WANTS

- To explain the reality of war.

- To reveal its raw humanity.

- To understand why it was that he was unable to pull the trigger.

☞ KEYWORDS   joy   destiny   beautiful

Nugget

❝ Wouldn't call it fear. This old mullah and a boy come up to the checkpoint once, the old fella's waving his arms and the lad's grinning, but mad like, pushing a wheelbarrow. There's a body, young woman, kid's mum by all accounts, and she's had her foot blown off by a mine. Must've seen me coming, eh? I walk over to patch her up and just as I get there the boy pulls something... a string or something... and I see a bag of explosives under the woman... in the barrow. Well, something went wrong, coz it just sort of smoked and went all runny and the smell... poor woman had shat herself. Just then the old mullah pulls out a pistol, but I'm quick so we're just standing there. Know he's a knacker, know my SA80 is going to drop him, but I couldn't... his eyes, he was smiling, like the old bastard was ready for it, looking for it, his death, shining he was, like one of them paintings of Jesus, a Saint or something, and I just felt this... I felt this... joy... this is it... our destiny, the old man, the young boy, his mum... and the British soldier. I was two inches in tomorrow's newspaper... but it was beautiful. Apart from the unholy stench. Stood there like that… felt like fifteen years. The old boy coughed – something come up out of his lung, spat it on the floor, put his pistol in his pocket, said something to the boy, turned his wheelbarrow… and walked away. Can't explain that to this day. **99**

Gilt

Stephen Greenhorn, Rona Munro and Isabel Wright

☞ **WHO**   Chris, Scottish, age is unspecified.

☞ **TO WHOM**   The audience (see note on 'Direct audience address' in the introduction).

☞ **WHERE**   Unspecified. Perhaps somewhere outside on the street or in a park. You decide.

☞ **WHEN**   Present day.

☞ **WHAT HAS JUST HAPPENED**   Chris has spent much of his life living on the streets. When we first meet him he is staying in a dingy flat with Jo, a teenage girl who is equally lost and alone. However, when Jo is given fifty thousand pounds by a man she has slept with in order that she keeps quiet about the affair, she moves out, leaving Chris on his own. He, meanwhile, has been running 'errands for the boys'. This has involved picking up bags in designated places and delivering them to Al who works in the bar of a hotel. On the last occasion, Chris, thinking there might be money in the bag, dared to look inside. To his horror he found a dead body hacked to pieces and covered in blood. Chris is repulsed by the sight of it and, once he has delivered the bag, makes a decision that this will be the very last time.

☞ **WHAT TO CONSIDER**

- The play follows the stories of seven people whose lives are strangely interwoven. Read the play to understand fully the intricacies of its plot and the complexity of its themes.

- The horror and repulsion he feels at having had a diced body in a bag in his possession.

- The strength of Chris's character. However down and out he might be, he refuses to lose his dignity or sense of morality.

- The ease with which a person can become homeless.

- 'Jaikie' is a word used to describe a tramp/an alcoholic/a down-and-out.

☞ WHAT HE WANTS

- To show that living rough is not synonymous with a loss of humanity.

- To justify his actions. He knows he has stepped over some line and is keen to explain how and why it could have happened.

- To challenge the smugness that our materialistic world engenders.

- To determine some moral ground for himself.

- To maintain his sense of self. How hard might this be if you have absolutely nothing? To what extent do most of us quantify and qualify ourselves according to what we have?

☞ KEYWORDS   meal   sleep   spiritual   bigger   scared   bottom   jungle   beasts

Chris

❝ When you've got your next meal and somewhere to sleep sorted, that's when you have time to ask the spiritual questions. Consider the bigger things in life.

First time I ended up on the street I was so scared, just young you know. Curled up in a doorway, shaking. Thought I was at the absolute bottom. I was out in the jungle and the beasts were coming to get me. Then you get to know folk. You just step round the trouble. Most folk would as soon be good to you as not, or else everyone's scared all the time aren't they? I'm no saying it's fucking *Les Mis*. But you'd never sleep if you spend every second waiting to get a brick through your head.

Thing is, you take what you can and you don't contemplate. You take the bag and don't ask who is so expendable they can be cut into steak-size pieces and got rid of. It's a world that lets folk drop off the edge of the radar. Naebody feels it. The lack. Doesnae keep naeb'dy awake if there's one less hoor on the streets, one less rent boy, if that old jaikie they pass every morning just vanishes overnight.

When you've a meal and a sleep sorted, that's when you have time to ask questions. (*Sarcastic*.) 'Am I truly satisfied? Do I have space to grow? I love my wife, but am I in love with her? How can I use my transferable skills to achieve my boyhood dream? Can I still be working class and rent a villa in Tuscany?'

Look, I always said don't look in the bag. That's the answer. See where curiosity gets you? Cannae do it anymore. I'd rather do the streets. 💬

God's Property

Arinze Kene

☞ **WHO**　　Chima, mixed race (Irish mother/Nigerian father), late twenties.

☞ **TO WHOM**　　Onochie, his brother, mid-teens.

☞ **WHERE**　　The kitchen of their family home, Deptford, South London.

☞ **WHEN**　　1982.

☞ **WHAT HAS JUST HAPPENED**　　Chima has just been released from prison having served a ten-year sentence for the murder of his white girlfriend, Poppy. For a few days he has been sleeping rough, before arriving back at the family home in Deptford, South London. At the start of the play, Chima enters through the back door with shopping bags full of food. There is no one in the kitchen. He calls out to his mother and, while he is upstairs looking for her, his younger brother, Onochie, arrives home. Onochie is surprised to find the back door open and the bags on the floor. He assumes that there is a burglar in the house, and when Chima comes downstairs Onochie threatens him with a knife. Onochie has not seen Chima since he was a small boy, so it takes Chima a while to convince Onochie that they are brothers. Chima is shocked to see that Onochie is now a 'skinhead', and, as the brothers slowly settle into a conversation, it is clear that, politically, the two young men are poles apart. Onochie has no interest in the struggles of his black 'brothers', many of whom are unemployed, have been rioting in Brixton, some even dying in police custody. While Onochie considers himself white, Chima has learned that, in the eyes of the world, he will only ever be regarded as black. Onochie then asks Chima about his time in prison. The speech that follows is Chima's response. Although he tells it in the third person, we can assume he is talking about himself.

☞ **WHAT TO CONSIDER**

- This speech is the set-up for a longer story in which Chima recalls how the 'white family' in prison betrayed him and how the 'black family' protected him. So make strong the warning: 'Dey'll let you know how black you are, bwoy.' It is portentous.

- The social and political background. Familiarise yourself with the events surrounding the Brixton riots, the New Cross Fire and 'Operation Swamp'.

- When you read the play, you'll discover that Poppy was in fact killed by her own father, and it was decided that, in order to protect Onochie, Chima should take the blame.

- Although at this point in the play Onochie is unaware of the fact, their mother has committed suicide. Chima has found a suicide note, which he tears up shortly after the speech.

- The struggles experienced by their Nigerian father, who eventually died of alcoholism, following dismissal from the Post Office for having a nose bleed. 'They didn't like that he bled everywhere'.

- 'Half-caste' is a derogatory term to describe people of mixed race and was in typical usage at the time.

☞ **WHAT HE WANTS**

- To illustrate his political standpoint.
- To educate Onochie.
- To protect Onochie.

☞ **KEYWORDS**   humbling   hard   fresh   innocence
family/families   half-caste   whites   blacks   choice/choose
unprotected   malice   disappointed

Chima

❝ This young guy. About your age. Comes through. He's fresh. He's still got the scent of innocence about him, only been there a week or whatever. Half-caste brother. Bit nervous. Now, when you come it's all about family – what family you're with – it's important. You understand – you gotta run with a unit, a gang or whatever. [...]

So it's the main block and in this building, to put it simply, you got about a hundred and twenty, a hundred and thirty inmates. But the main two families are the whites and the blacks, right? The whites and the blacks – and they don't seem to like each other very much – similar to here in Deptford. Now, as I said, this half-caste brother, he's in the middle, half'n'half. He's smart though, he knows that he cannot be with both – he has to make a choice or that leaves him unprotected in there. You don't wanna be unprotected in there. Both families are looking at him like 'Where you gonna go, kid, where you gonna go?'

He gets familiar with these white guys – [...]

In particular there's four of them he's knocking elbows with. They're always together – in the canteen, on the grounds, in study, in the chapel, everything, that's his little posse – they're all right – he cracks a smile for the first time since he's been inside. But see, every time this half-caste guy looks over his shoulder in the canteen, on the grounds, walking back to his cell, wherever, every time he looks over his shoulder, he seems to lock eyes with black guys from the other family, they're watching him. Shaking their head at him, no malice – it's just as though... they're disappointed. He doesn't know why, cos the way he sees it, he's both black *and* white. He can choose. [...] Who the fuck are they to... [...]

You know?

So. Wet rainy afternoon. Out on the grounds playing footy is half-caste and his four chums. One of them loses control of the football and it rolls off the pitch. The ball goes straight to the blacks congregating in a group there by the bench. Half-caste is not intimidated by this. From where he stood, he says: 'Oi. Pass it 'ere.' Well, the big blackies – some of them with dreadlocks – they're amused by this. They laugh at him, like he's a child, and they absolutely do not pass him the ball. Half-caste walks over, still cocky, like. He bends to pick up the ball and by when he stands back up, what's he got? Towering over him, a black man. Black man says (*Thick Jamaican accent*):

'Dey'll let you know.'

Half-caste – 'You what?'

'Dey'll let you know how black you are, bwoy.' **99**

Holes in the Skin

Robert Holman

☞ **WHO**   Lee, eighteen, from Stokesley, North Yorkshire.

☞ **TO WHOM**   Kerry, fifteen, and her mother, Hazel.

☞ **WHERE**   Hazel and Kerry's house on a council estate in Stokesley.

☞ **WHEN**   Present day.

☞ **WHAT HAS JUST HAPPENED**   Kerry and her mother Hazel have moved to a house on a council estate a few doors down from where Lee and his brother Ewan live. Kerry has asked Ewan to beat up her mother's new boyfriend Dennis, whom she hates. Ewan does so, but gets carried away and Dennis dies in the attack. As soon as Lee finds out, he rushes to Kerry's house looking for Ewan. He is scared that the police will come looking for him and Ewan. Lee is the first person the police suspect if there is trouble. He has been in a young offenders' prison. Kerry asks him what it was he did. The speech that follows is his response to her.

☞ **WHAT TO CONSIDER**

- Lee is described variously as 'a good lad' and 'His nature is to be bad'. You decide.

- Lee is attracted to Kerry.

- Lee is addicted to heroin.

- Lee's mother is an alcoholic.

- Freya is a teacher who lives in a neighbouring village. She has taken Lee under her wing. Read the play to discover more about their unusual relationship.

- Deerbolt is a young offenders' establishment in County Durham.

☞ **WHAT HE WANTS**

- To set the record straight.

- To elicit sympathy.

- For Kerry to fancy him.

☞ KEYWORDS   fracas *(is this his choice of word or was it the word used in court?)*   unfortunately   accident   guilty   intent   consequences   antecedence   slippery   dangerous   impudence

Lee

❝ I didn't mean to do it. I had a fracas with a schoolkid once. [I broke his neck] […] Unfortunately for me. I suppose more unfortunately for him actually. I pushed him off a wall. It was an accident. He overbalanced. They said I pushed him, but I didn't really. I got four years for it. I was guilty of GBH with intent. I didn't intend. They said I should have foresaw the consequences. I was fifteen. The boy was eleven. A lot was made of that in court with the judge and the jury and everything. That's what swung it against us. Also I looked older by the time I came to court. The lad was in a wheelchair which didn't help us. All the sympathy was bound to be with him. And when my antecedence was read out I'd got shoplifting charges, and cautions and all that. The judge said he'd no choice but to send me down. He said I was on a slippery slope and a very dangerous young man. I wasn't a young man. I was a kid who'd just done something on the spur of the moment for no reason. The only person who cared was Freya. Freya came to court with us every day. They sent me mam away for shouting at the little boy when he was giving his evidence. The judge told the jury they had to disregard her impudence. How could they? He didn't when he sentenced me, after he'd read all the reports. I could tell he didn't like us, he made it very clear. He ignored the psychiatrist who said a long prison sentence wasn't the best option for us. I was already being bullied in Deerbolt, so I know what he meant. It was me who'd told him anyway. I told him I'd been raped by two bully boys in the showers, one after the other, and one who just watched and didn't do it. I told him I wasn't coping at all well. ❞

Invisible

Tena Štivičić

☞ **WHO**   Felix, thirty-five, a businessman.

☞ **TO WHOM**   His therapist.

☞ **WHERE**   In a therapy consultation room.

☞ **WHEN**   The middle of the first decade of the twenty-first century.

☞ **WHAT HAS JUST HAPPENED**   Felix, an outwardly successful businessman, is married to Ann. Felix wants to have a child, but Ann is worried it will interfere with her career as a nutritionist. They have stopped having sex. Felix is unhappy and has sought the help of a therapist. In the speech that follows he tries to explain his depression.

☞ **WHAT TO CONSIDER**

- Felix works for a company that builds wind farms. These are the 'turbines' to which he refers.

- Felix suppresses a lot of anger over which, when it erupts, he has no control.

☞ **WHAT HE WANTS**

- To articulate what he is feeling. Notice how he struggles to find the words.

- To be heard and to be understood.

- To recapture that moment of happiness.

- Reassurance that he is not a bad person.

☞ **KEYWORDS**   sink   miserable   gloomy   despairing struggling   tears   tired   happy   dream/dreams beautiful/beauty   dissolved   pathetic

Felix

❝ I would look at those turbines and they seemed like blenders to me. Like I'm stuck in some kind of… dough and it's revolving really fast and I'm in it right up to my chin and I can't come out.

He trails off, struggling to find words.

I find it difficult to feel happy. If I'm on my own, I find it difficult not to sink. Being around other people tends to lift my spirits. But then, I suspect that might be simply because I'm too insecure to let them see the real me. The miserable, gloomy, despairing me. I feel confused a lot of the time as to what my goal is in life. I can work sixteen hours a day but then simple tasks, simple obstacles like having to speak to a phone company or going around roadworks… or Tube delays or… or even struggling to open a bag of nuts can bring me to the verge of tears. I wait for the weekend to have a life and then I can't get it together to get out of bed.

Every… every so often… on a regular basis… I need to remind myself of the good things in life. Health, income, a loving partner, a comfortable home, living in the most exciting city in the world. You tire of London, you tire of life, isn't that how the saying goes? Well… of course I'm not tired, I'm thirty-five. How can I be tired?

So I remind myself how all of this could be gone in a second, I could be diagnosed with some terrible illness tomorrow. Which I'm sure I will be. That makes it even harder. That makes me feel like I really really need to grab these times by the horns… and I feel like… sleeping.

Sometimes I'm happy in my dreams. I remember there was this one dream. I was in a cottage, somewhere that resembled Switzerland. Never-ending green and deep clear water. It was the most beautiful… I can't explain to you how beautiful it was. Maybe that's how beauty feels when you're happy. There was a woman. It wasn't Ann. It was a woman I didn't know and yet she felt familiar. She came up to the porch, she was carrying a bunch of bright wild flowers. And she gave them to me and she said: 'I love you.' I don't think I have ever felt that intensely happy in my whole life as I did in that dream. And in those few seconds when I woke up before it dissolved.

Am I not the most pathetic man? **99**

Japes
Simon Gray

☞ **WHO**   Michael, mid-twenties, middle-class, a writer.

☞ **TO WHOM**   Jason, his younger brother.

☞ **WHERE**   The sitting room of their house in Hampstead, North London.

☞ **WHEN**   The early 1970s.

☞ **WHAT HAS JUST HAPPENED**   Michael and Jason's parents are dead. The young men have shared ownership of the house they grew up in and where they continue to live. Here, close to the start of the play, they have been discussing Michael's girlfriend Anita. Michael has asked Jason whether he minds the fact that she has been staying the night. Michael admits that he himself does not like the smell of the pot that Anita smokes. The speech that follows comes as a response to Jason asking, 'But you haven't said anything to her have you?'

☞ WHAT TO CONSIDER

- Michael is a writer. Throughout the play he is keen to find words that best describe his emotions.

- Jason, whose nickname is 'Japes', is crippled. It happened following a childhood accident when the two boys were playing on a diving board. Michael blames himself.

- Michael wants to marry Anita. It will mean changes to the way they have been living.

- Michael is already guilty about the accident, which he believes to have been his fault. The prospect of turfing Jason out of the family home to make room for his wife is something that worries Michael.

- Jason has also been sleeping with Anita.

- The play spans twenty-seven years, charting the relationship between the brothers and their shared love for Anita.

- The speech is short, but allows for a deal of emotional scope.

☞ WHAT HE WANTS

- To understand his growing feelings for Anita.
- To articulate these feelings.
- To explain to Jason why he needs to have Anita in the house.
- Jason's approval.

☞ KEYWORDS   worries/worrying/worry   thinking   mystery
who

Michael

❝ The point is she's not – she hasn't – well, she's still a guest. So of course I haven't said anything. But I might. Soon. That's the point. But what worries me is – is that I've started worrying about her. I mean, when I should be working I start thinking, thinking, well, she ought to be bloody here by now, and where is she, and then a sort of worry grows, just a little one, never specific, not about her being run over or assaulted or – meeting somebody else, for God's sakes, least of all that – it's more – a worry over the mystery of her – of who she is. That's what worries me about her absence, her lateness – not where or what or why – but who. Who is she? Perhaps the point is – the real point is – that I'm in love with her. Never felt like that about any of the others. Have you ever known me feel like that? **❞**

Jerusalem
Jez Butterworth

☞ **WHO**   Davey, a young man, from the fictional village of
Flintock in Wiltshire.

☞ **TO WHOM**   Lee, his friend.

☞ **WHERE**   A clearing in the wood on the outskirts of Flintock
where Johnny 'Rooster' Byron lives.

☞ **WHEN**   Present day, St George's Day.

☞ **WHAT HAS JUST HAPPENED**   The play tells the story of Johnny
'Rooster' Byron, delightful rogue and maverick, a Pied Piper for
our times. He lives in a caravan on the edge of the village. The
local youth flock to him. He sells them drugs and gives them
alcohol, offering them a safe place to party and to hang out.
Davey is one of the group, along with his good friend Lee. Today
is St George's Day, and the Flintock Fair is in full swing. Meanwhile,
Johnny has been given only hours to vacate his caravan before
the local council mean to bulldoze it. Lee, who is set to leave for
Australia at six the following morning, has come with Davey to
say goodbye to Rooster. Davey says to Lee, 'You ready for your
dream quest then?' and asks him 'Why do you want to change
your name?' As Lee tries to explain his need to travel he quizzes
Davey about whether he too has wanted to be more than just
'David Dean from Flintock'. The speech that follows is Davey's
response to Lee's imminent departure.

☞ **WHAT TO CONSIDER**

- Davey is rooted in Wiltshire. In an earlier exchange, he
  expresses disgust at the way local news stations report events
  as far away as Gloucestershire. It is humourous, but gives an
  insight into the love he has for his particular region and also
  the fear he feels at the prospect of anything remotely foreign.

- After the speech, Lee says to Davey, 'You're going to live your
  whole life with the same fucking people, going to the same
  shit pubs, kill two million cows, and die a sad, fat povvo.' Davey

is not offended. As far as he is concerned, life is all about money and sex.

- As they go to leave, Davey instructs Lee to smell the air. It is beautiful English air heralding the arrival of summer.

- Find a balance in your characterisation between Davey's crudeness and his sweet sensitivity.

- 'Hazmat' is a contraction of 'hazardous materials' and means Davey has to wear protective clothing at work.

☞ WHAT HE WANTS

- To assert himself. (by explaining to Lee that he is happy with his life).

- To make Lee see that the world is essentially the same all over.

- To entertain Lee. Davey cannot help but play the clown.

☞ KEYWORDS   wham   slay   shag   quest

Davey

❝ My name's David Dean. I work in the abattoir. Get there six in the morning – hungover, hazmat suit, goggles – and I stand there and I slay two hundred cows. Wham. Next contestant. What's your name and where d'you come from? (*Mimes killing a cow.*) Wham! Have lunch. Pot Noodle. Come back. Slay two hundred more. End of the week, I walk out of there. I'll tell you what I ain't thinking. I ain't thinking: 'Perhaps I'll change my name. Get a Celtic tattoo. See this on my arse? That symbolises the Harmony of the Spheres. That's Vishnu, God of Gayness.' I'll tell you what I'm thinking: 'Shag on. It's the weekend. Pay me. Show me the paper, and shag on.' I wish you well on your quest, Frodo. But whatever you change your name to, you're still fucking Lee Piper; and wherever you go in this world, when you get off the plane, boat, train or crawl out of the jungle smeared in paint, the bloke waiting to meet you is also called Lee Piper. Make paper. Make more paper. Shag on. ❞

Jonah and Otto

Robert Holman

☞ **WHO**   Jonah Teale, twenty-six, from Knutsford in Cheshire.

☞ **TO WHOM**   Otto Banister, sixty-two, a clergyman.

☞ **WHERE**   An area of open ground on the East Sussex coast.

☞ **WHEN**   Present day, summer.

☞ **WHAT HAS JUST HAPPENED**   The play tells the story of a chance meeting between Jonah, a young man waiting with his baby daughter for the midnight ferry to France, and Otto, a sixty-two-year-old clergyman. Jonah happens across Otto in a secluded public garden late one summer night. Jonah is dressed in a hoody, and at first it seems as though he is going to rob Otto. However, as the story proceeds, we realise that Jonah is gentle, and, as the two men talk about their loves and losses, we learn more and more about them. In this scene they have moved from the garden to an open area of land. It is the following day and Otto is asking Jonah about his father. The speech that follows is made up of Jonah's response.

☞ **WHAT TO CONSIDER**

- Jonah suffers from epilepsy.

- He studied English at Hull University.

- His best friend committed suicide when he was thirteen.

- Jonah is something of a magician and enjoys card tricks.

- His girlfriend and the mother of his six-week-old daughter is French. Her name is Emilie.

- The men spend just under twenty-four hours together. They form a bond and develop a friendship that is out of the ordinary. Read the play to understand fully its mysterious nature.

- In many ways, Otto becomes a surrogate father to Jonah, and Jonah in turn takes on the role of the son that Otto always wanted.

- Both men feel a pressure to be the absolute best they can be.

☞ **WHAT HE WANTS**

- To share his pain.
- To find relief from his loneliness.
- Sympathy.

☞ **KEYWORDS**   Heaven   hell   good   cried   hate

☞ **NB**   This play offers a number of other speeches from which to choose.

Jonah

❝ There's nothing to say really. He climbed the ladder to Heaven when I was a child. […] He got cancer. He had bowel cancer. He farted a lot, then he passed away. All in about nine months. I was only nine. Nines are everywhere. That's the other thing I had to have done. I had to have a colonoscopy. I wouldn't have minded really, but all the students had to look up my bum as well. […]

It's not funny. […]

He was the best dad in the world.

[…] He was only forty-six. I missed him like hell. I used to go to my mum, and try and be good an' that. I used to really try. I used to bake. To be extremely honest with you, I could make cakes and stuff. I used to do little butterfly buns with a Smartie on top as an extra. She did her best to cover up. I wish she hadn't really. I wish we'd all sat down and cried. My mum had two miscarriages between my brother Richard and me. It's why he's a bit older. I don't know why I'm telling you this. Except it made a difference really. My mum told me what it was like to lose two children. So I always felt a bit responsible. I always felt I had to try really hard. You said there must be something funny in the family. There isn't. My sister's at college. She's going to be a doctor. The only thing that's funny is that I'm the thick one. And my mum. She teaches infants. She works hard for us all. I do my best not to be private with her. Except I am a touch. I wasn't as a boy. It just got that way as I grew up. I know it hurts her a little bit when I don't say much sometimes. I do try. I think you have to have one of your parents pass away, for you to sit down and talk to the other one. The trouble is, my dad passed away when I was too young for it to be possible. I hate him for that. I don't. I hate him for dying. I'd know my mum better if he hadn't died. It's odd. It should be the opposite. It isn't. **99**

Ladies Down Under

Amanda Whittington

☞ **WHO**   Shane, Australian, a surfer. His age is unspecified, but we assume in his twenties or early thirties.

☞ **TO WHOM**   Charlie, an ageing English hippy.

☞ **WHERE**   Surfers Paradise, Queensland, Australia.

☞ **WHEN**   February 2007.

☞ **WHAT HAS JUST HAPPENED**   *Ladies Down Under* is the sequel to *Ladies' Day*, in which four female fish-factory workers from Hull win a small fortune at the races. One and a half years on they have booked a holiday to Sydney, Australia. However, when Jan's boyfriend Joe fails to meet them at the airport they decide to change their plans and head further afield. Here on Queensland's Gold Coast they meet Shane, who delivers the speech that follows.

☞ **WHAT TO CONSIDER**

- We know very little about Shane other than that he is a typical 'surfer dude'.

- It is a comic speech and you can be bold in your characterisation. Have fun with it.

- He is talking to Charlie, who is stoned. In the play Charlie plays the bongos as Shane speaks, which heightens the drama of Shane's story.

☞ **WHAT HE WANTS**

- To luxuriate in the sensory pleasures that surfing affords him. Note how even the anticipation of riding the waves is pleasure enough.

- To prove how tough he is.

- To boast how fearless he is.

- To strut his stuff like a peacock. Decide to what extent he believes he has superhuman strength.

☞ KEYWORDS   waiting   broken   steal   score   regret
respect   shredding   overhead-plus   scratching   rips   stingers
sharks   plunging   hyenas   Paradise

Shane

❝ Fresh board wax – the most beautiful smell in the world.
It's all you need on a day like today: the sun on your back, the
sand at your feet and the waves out there waiting. Call me a
beach bum if it makes you feel better, but I know what I am. I
know who I am. Me and my mates, we've come down since we
were kids. We've broken boards and bones, and not just our
own. When the tourists come to steal the waves, we let 'em
know the score. Drop in on us and you'll regret it, mate.
That's how it goes down here: to get respect you gotta give it.
And the ocean gets the most respect of all. […] Yesterday, I
see my mate shredding one from the back and it's just like a
movie, only better. Then a double overhead-plus set appears
on the horizon. It's coming for us and coming fast. I thought
'This is it, Shane. This time you've bought it for sure.' We're
out there scratching for our lives. We're making the waves by
the skin of our teeth but then the rips go against us, we lose
our boards and we're down in the water with the stingers and
the sharks. A plunging wave pulls us under but somehow we
push through. We're home and dry. Lying in the sand and
laughing like hyenas, and back to do it all again today. […]
Surfers Paradise, for sure. **❞**

Lagan

Stacey Gregg

☞ **WHO** Ian, twenty-four, from Belfast.

☞ **TO WHOM** The audience (see note on 'Direct audience address' in the introduction).

☞ **WHERE** On a ferry from Holyhead to Dublin and a train from Dublin to Belfast.

☞ **WHEN** Present day.

☞ **WHAT HAS JUST HAPPENED** The play tells the story of ten interrelated characters from Belfast. The Lagan is the river that flows through the city. This speech comes at the very start of the play and charts Ian's journey from England back home to Belfast.

☞ **WHAT TO CONSIDER**

- Ian has moved away from home and is living in London with his lover Stefan. Stefan was his German tutor.

- Ian has not come out to his parents but is eager to do so.

- He has spent a year in Africa and considers himself well travelled.

- Having moved away from home he is very critical of Belfast's small-town ways.

- He is described as having 'airs and graces' and thinking he is better than others. Note how judgemental he is about the strangers on his journey. Decide to what extent he is a snob and to what extent this is borne out of his own fear of inadequacy and insignificance.

- Decide to what extent he has a love/hate relationship to home. By the end of the play he chooses to stay in Belfast for a while.

- His mother says of him: 'Looking awful Londony. Wish he'd cut his hair.'

- He wears tweed and carries a man bag.

- He has a teenage sister called Aoife who is pregnant and wants an abortion. She is the reason for the 'cryptic summons'.

- A kraken is a legendary gigantic sea monster.

- Aoife is pronounced 'Eefa'.

☞ WHAT HE WANTS

- To protect himself. By casting himself in the role of the 'romantic traveller' and noting his journey as a poet might, he copes with his fear of returning home. Note how he needs to distance himself from the ordinary people on the boat and train and how he refuses to make the journey by air, where there is very little opportunity for poetic reflection and where passengers are herded like cattle.

☞ KEYWORDS   mysterious   undulating   beautiful   barren   divorced   primitive

Ian

❝ sea behind, lean against peeling iron, salt and rust, – deck lunges, knees absorb, spray sticky on my cheek.

Someone lights a smoke. (*Miffed.*) There's only two decks, and this is not the designated smokers' area, actually.

(*Posturing, a bit grand.*) Never waste the crossing faffing round arcades or queuing for Fanta. Always spend it up here, *mysterious*, – the roar of the engine and the horizon, the upturned bowl of sky, – (*Spotting something.*) seabird! Undulating M, soaring, clockless, – (*Looking down.*) imagine the eye of a kraken, staring back up through the ocean swell…

Pulls out his notebook. Scribbles.

'Undulating M.' That's a keeper.

[…]

Dublin appears, black against low cloud, ghostly. My hands, brown against the hard white light – mad she'll think me for not just flying back to Belfast from London. God knows what's up. I'll take my time sure. Sure I've long passed caring for the relentless advice. Mother's cryptic summons, pfft – she's not the boss of me, takin my time so I am, happy to take the Holyhead ferry to Dublin, the two-hour train / north.

[…]

Skanger swaggers out. Drops a carton at his arse. People actually behave like that. Maybe I've been away too long […]

Wonder how my sister is. Wee Aoife. Seventeen now? Mad. Haven't been home enough. Haven't been back best part of a year. Before that, nearly a year again. Too often if you ask me. I'm over it. Home…

Crew prop open one door and we bottleneck, obedient, till some Irish voice mutters 'somethin somethin the other bloody door.' Spill onto the walkway, catch the Dart to Connelly Station.

[…]

On the train to Belfast there's a wee woman keeps trying to trick me into conversation, but I'm not havin it. Some old-boys' club banterin the girl serving tea. Woman opposite rolls her eyes. Ironic: find her just as irritating.

[…]

Cross the border. I know cos my mobile buzzes with the change in network. Farmland and scrag smudge by in silent hurry. Love this journey. Weird. Something about zooming through the barren, littered land. I've travelled a fair bit, actually, and the natural Ireland is divorced, irrevocably divorced from the urban. The natural Ireland is – answers something no other landscape can replace. Can't explain it. Maybe – maybe it is just recognition of the landscape of memory, childhood. Or maybe it's something more primitive, in the blood and bone of me…

'Irrevocably divorced.' That's good.

He scribbles it down. 〃

Little Baby Jesus

Arinze Kene

☞ **WHO**   Kehinde, sixteen, black, from London.

☞ **TO WHOM**   The audience (see note on 'Direct audience address' in the introduction).

☞ **WHERE**   Inner-city London. Exact location is unspecified. Perhaps you imagine him talking to us in his bedroom, a street or the park.

☞ **WHEN**   Present day.

☞ **WHAT HAS JUST HAPPENED**   The play, a series of interconnected monologues, describes the point at which three teenagers, Kehinde, Joanne and Rugrat, begin to grow up. They speak directly to the audience, and in this, Kehinde's first monologue, he introduces himself.

☞ **WHAT TO CONSIDER**

- Kehinde is British of Nigerian descent.

- He is described as 'mature', 'very sensible for his age', with 'a sensitivity about him; an innocence'.

- His grandmother has strong views on colour and race. In Kehinde's next monologue he tells us about how she attacked his brother's white girlfriend.

- Kehinde has a twin: a girl called 'Taiwo' to whom he is very close. Read the play to find out what happens to her.

- 'Oyinbo' means 'white'. 'Pehpeh' means 'breasts'.

☞ **WHAT HE WANTS**

- To introduce himself. Note how closely he identifies himself with race and racial issues.

- To apologise for having hated the way 'God' made him.

- To express and share with us his own understanding of how immature he was and how he knows he needs to change and grow up.

☞ **KEYWORDS** mixed-race obsessive traded shameful compensate oyinbo

☞ **NB** This play offers a number of other speeches from which to choose.

Kehinde

❝ I used to have 'mixed-raced-girl syndrome'. Mixed-race-girl syndrome is the long obsessive phase of over-fancying mixed-race girls. Girls of that lighter complexion. Most guys get it when they're like fourteen, fifteen. My favourite was when that black African or Caribbean skin mixes with that white English or European skin. You get that sun-kissed finish.

At one point. I actually wanted to be mixed-race. I wished for it. I wished my hair wouldn't curl over itself like pepper grains, I wanted it to be bouncy and coolie. But no, broom bristles instead I concluded I was stuck with. I'd gladly have traded this nose for one that was sharper at the end. Shameful, I know. I was so stupid, I got down one time, asked God to forgive me for my sins, to protect my family and to bless me with pink lips. I actually remember going to sleep wishing that I'd wake up with green eyes.

My prayers were obviously ignored and I didn't turn into a mixed-raced boy. And if I were God I would've blanked me for a year just to chastise me for being so ungrateful of this beautiful black skin I was gifted with – Praise God. Believe I had a lot of growing up to do.

Well, I couldn't have grown up all that quick though because next I got a really light-skinned girlfriend. I just couldn't leave the lighties alone. Said, if I couldn't be one, I'd have to represent one – to compensate.

My grandma calls it 'Yellow Fever'. She said it all started around slavery times when white overseers would secretly admire the beauty. I'm sure that back then it was nothing to rape black women. Africa was like the white man's back garden and he did whatever he saw fit with his fruit. She said it's not our fault though, she says something's wrong with us. She always used to say –

(*Nigerian accent.*) '*You African men are magnet for oyinbo pehpeh too much. You de follow-follow and think you are among dem but they will let you know how black you are. IF you trust a white man to build the ceiling above your head, you mustn't complain of neck problems, my child, na your fault be dat!*'

If I bring home a girl who's any bit lighter than me then –

'*Ah-Kehinde! It's getting late, your oyinbo friend has to go home. Doesn't she have a home or have her parents split up?*'

Cos all white people's parents are divorced according to Grandma.

My older brother, he would sneak girls into the house all the time. When Grandma would go by his room, he'd get the girl to hide down on the side of the bed, on the floor. **99**

Love and Information

Caryl Churchill

☞ **WHO**   Unspecified.

☞ **TO WHOM**   Unspecified.

☞ **WHERE**   Unspecified. You decide.

☞ **WHEN**   Present day.

☞ **WHAT HAS JUST HAPPENED**   This monologue, entitled 'The Child Who Didn't Know Fear', is one of over seventy short scenes that go to make up Caryl Churchill's full-length play *Love and Information*.

☞ **WHAT TO CONSIDER**

- The play is in seven sections. Within the sections there are several scenes. These scenes can be played in any order. There is no indication about what age or sex the characters are, other than the content of what is written. Here, the speaker could be a man or a woman. All we have to go on is a stage direction that reads: '*One person tells a story to another.*'

- Arguably, it is an unusual piece for an audition. However, if you are looking for something that shows off your storytelling skills (perhaps you are auditioning for the role of a narrator), or you need material for a voice showreel, then, I suggest, it would make an excellent choice.

- Use the opportunity to create a character for yourself and make a decision about to whom exactly you are speaking. How would it differ if you were talking to a stranger/friend/lover/partner/wife?

- Create a context for yourself. Perhaps the speech is serving to make a wider point within a relationship.

- What is the moral of the tale?

- Look for ways of animating the speech. For example, how might the child and children speak?

- Within the play there are over one hundred voices all trying to cope with an information overload.

☞ WHAT HE WANTS

- To humour the listener.
- To warn the listener.
- To instruct the listener.

☞ KEYWORDS   fear   shiver   tingle   creeps   shudder
haunted   frightened   dead   monster   screams

Unspecified

" *One person tells a story to another.*

Once upon a time there was a child who didn't know what fear was and he wanted to find out. So his friends said, Cold shiver down your back, legs go funny, sometimes your hands no not your hands yes your hands tingle, it's more in your head, it's in your stomach, your belly you shit yourself, you can't breathe, your skin your skin creeps, it's a shiver a shudder do you really not know what it is? And the child said, I don't know what you mean. So they took him to a big dark empty house everyone said was haunted. They said, No one's ever been able to stay here till morning, you won't stay till midnight, you won't last a hour, and the child said, Why, what's going to happen? And they said, You'll know what we mean about being frightened. And the child said, Good, that's what I want to know. So in the morning his friends came back and there was the child sitting in the dusty room. And they said, You're still here? what happened? And the child said, There were things walking about, dead things, some of them didn't have heads and a monster with glowing – and his friends said, Didn't you run away? and the child said, There were weird noises like screams and like music but not music, and his friends said, What did you feel? and the child said, It came right up to me and put out its hand, and his friends said, Didn't your hair your stomach the back of your neck your legs weren't you frightened? And the child said, No, it's no good, I didn't feel anything, I still don't know what fear is. And on the way home he met a lion and the lion ate him. **99**

Misterman

Enda Walsh

☞ **WHO**   Thomas Magill, thirty-three, Irish.

☞ **TO WHOM**   His dead father.

☞ **WHERE**   His father's grave, in Inishfree, a fictional small town in rural Ireland.

☞ **WHEN**   Present day.

☞ **WHAT HAS JUST HAPPENED**   The play tells the story of Thomas Magill. It is a one-man show in which other characters are played by Thomas himself or are played to us from tape recordings. Thomas lives in Inishfree, Ireland, a place, he says, whose 'pure white soul [is] being stained by the bad'. Thomas is convinced that God has chosen him to bring salvation to his sinful neighbours, and as he goes about his daily business we meet them through his eyes. Here, Thomas, on his way to buying biscuits for his mother, has come to visit the grave of his dead father, former grocery-shop owner.

☞ **WHAT TO CONSIDER**

- The heightened style of the play, its theatricality, its black humour and its exploration of dark and violent themes.

- The complexity of Thomas's character. He is very much the anti-hero. He is emotionally unstable. We are both captivated and appalled by him.

- Later in the play he will smash up his friend's garage, kick a dog to death and murder a fourteen-year-old girl.

- His father was also violent. His relationship with his mother is disturbing.

☞ **WHAT HE WANTS**

- To talk to his father as if he were still alive.

- To find a way of coping with the pain of his loss.

- To be heard. Throughout the play he complains that no one is listening.

☞ **KEYWORDS**   smashing   dynamite   avail   awkward
jangling   miss   quiet   terrible   curse

☞ **NB**   This play offers a number of other speeches from
which to choose.

Thomas

❝ Hello, Daddy, it's only me, Thomas. I just popped out to
get the mammy the bickies – I thought I'd check in with ya.
(*Slight pause.*) The grave's looking smashing, by the way! It's
the best of the lot, I'd say! Hey, what do you make of the
gravel map of Ireland on the drowning sea? It's dynamite, isn't
it, Daddy?! A good joke. A-one!

THOMAS *kneels down at his daddy's grave and lays the flowers
on it.*

So! Mickie-Joe-Goblin-McAllister's been banned from the
community centre for life, Daddy. A physio woman from out
of town had a weekend clinic for the elderly. There was all
manner of crippled people queuing down the road to avail of
her healing hands. I had thought of bringing Mammy but she
said she'd feel very awkward about another woman feeling her
up. Not so Mickie-Joe. Apparently he walked in, dropped his
knickers, said he had a chest infection and might he have a
suck of a lozenge.

A slight pause.

He's not half as funny as he makes himself out to be. In my
mind he's just a grubby little midget with a very long name –
though that can go a long way in Inishfree.

[…]

Billy Traynor got himself a new car, Daddy! Who's to say
there's no money in shovelling S-H-I-T! He's as proud as
punch just like the fella on the Lotto ad! Hey, will ya ever
forget the day ya caught him pinching the newspaper in our
shop, Daddy? Ya gave him an awful hiding that day! He was in

bits that night in Boyle's! Pouring the pints inta him to ease
the pain! Billy's only an old thief anyway! Everyone knows
that. No doubt he'll be at the dance tonight, jangling those
new car keys at the young girls, God help them.

A pause.

I really miss ya, Daddy. But I'm doing my best with it and I
bet you'd be proud of the work I'm doing about town too. It's
just funny not having the shop… and it being so quiet about
the house with Mammy and me and Trixie. The swelling's
gone down after the kittens, by the way. Mammy asked me to
drown three of them and keep the best one. 'Best to drown the
lot,' I said. Being an only child is tough… being an only kitten
in a town full of dogs would be a terrible curse though. It
really would. **"**

Mogadishu

Vivienne Franzmann

☞ **WHO**   Chuggs, fifteen, black, from London.

☞ **TO WHOM**   Saif, fifteen, his best friend, Asian Muslim.

☞ **WHERE**   Under the stairs in a school in London.

☞ **WHEN**   Present day.

☞ **WHAT HAS JUST HAPPENED**   Chuggs is part of Jason's gang. At the very start of the play they are in their snug, a small space under the stairs at school where they go to smoke weed. As they are laughing and messing about, a Turkish boy, Firat, passes by and accidentally knocks into Jason, causing Jason to burn a hole in his own shirt from his joint. The gang set about Firat, racially abusing him, and Jason pushes him to the ground. As he attempts to beat Firat further, Amanda, a teacher, appears and tries to intervene. Jason, who is by now consumed with anger, pushes her out of the way, and she falls to the floor. There is a distinct change in atmosphere as Jason registers what he has done. Without saying anything he and the other gang members walk coolly away as if nothing has happened. The following day Amanda goes to see the headmaster but is loath to make a formal complaint. She knows it could result in Jason's permanent exclusion from school, and she wants to prevent this. In the next scene, from which the speech that follows is taken, we are back under the stairs where Chuggs and Saif are smoking a spliff.

☞ **WHAT TO CONSIDER**

- Chuggs is often the butt of jokes.
- He is not as quick-witted as the others and is sometimes slow to understand.
- He is highly sensitive, and later on in the play he feels forced to defend himself. He tells Saif, 'You always think you's better than me. You's always takin' the piss. You's think I don't know, cos you think I'm so fuckin' thick. Well, I ain't.'

- His backstory. We do not know much about Chuggs' life outside school and the gang. You may like to use this opportunity to build a fully rounded character for yourself, making up details about his family and experiences. Beware of playing him as a stereotype.

☞ WHAT HE WANTS

- To entertain and to impress Saif.
- To show his intelligence over Emmanuel.
- To prove to Saif that he is not thick.

☞ KEYWORDS   steaming   proper   crease   sick

Chuggs

❝ So we's outside Chickstop and she comes steaming over. […] She goes, 'Whose dog is this?' And I go, 'What's it got to do with you?' And she gets this badge out and goes, 'I am an RSPCA inspector.' So I goes, 'It's my mum's.' She goes, 'What's it called?' And I go, 'Jackie Chan'. And she goes, 'What breed is it?' And I go, 'Japanese Akita Inu.' And she goes, 'That's a very expensive breed.' So I goes, 'What you tryin' to say?' And she goes, 'I'm just sayin' it's a very expensive breed.' And then Emmanuel comes out with Tyson who jumps up at her. And starts going proper mad at her. Like proper going at her, like it wants to kill her. And Emmanuel is laughin' and Tyson's got all this spit and shit round his mouth and every time Emmanuel pulls him back, he jumps back at her. And I'm tryin' to tell him that she the RSPCA lady. And she goes, 'He needs a muzzle.' And DeShaun goes, 'What about the dog?' And I crease, man. It was sick, man. And she gets that badge out again and shows Emmanuel and tells him she from the RSPCA and he needs to control his dog. And Tyson's still going for her. And Emmanuel shits himself and thinks the RSPCA lady will take Tyson if he don't control it so he gets this stick and starts hittin' him round the face. It was well bad. **❞**

Mother Teresa is Dead

Helen Edmundson

☞ **WHO** Mark, early thirties, strong London accent, white.

☞ **TO WHOM** Jane, late twenties, his wife.

☞ **WHERE** The living room of Frances's house in a village near Chennai, India.

☞ **WHEN** Present day.

☞ **WHAT HAS JUST HAPPENED** Before the play starts, Jane, having left her husband Mark and five-year-old son Joe without warning, has been travelling around India compelled to help those in need. When she arrives at Chennai Central Station she meets Srinivas, an Oxford-educated Indian man (to whom she is attracted), and goes to work in his shelter for street children. She is also taken in by Frances, a middle-aged English woman, an artist, who offers her somewhere to stay. Frances is worried about Jane. She has been clinging on to a white plastic carrier bag in which she says there is a baby. She is clearly disturbed. The play starts with Mark's arrival at Frances's house. Jane has asked Frances to contact Mark, and he has travelled from London in order to take her back home. Jane has been absent for seven weeks, and Mark wants to know why she left. She asks him if he has brought Joe with him. The speech that follows is made up of Mark's share of their conversation.

☞ **WHAT TO CONSIDER**

- Mark's inability to understand why Jane has needed to do what she has done. He holds the view that charity begins at home.

- Mark expresses sexist and racist views. Be careful that you do not play him as a stereotype. It is important that we understand (if not agree with) his point of view.

- He loves Jane and adores his son.

- He is unable to cope with Jane's depression.

- He is fearful.
- He is also vulnerable.
- His jealousy is not altogether unfounded. He rightly suspects Srinivas of stealing his wife's affections.
- Read the play to find out whether Jane returns with Mark or decides to stay in India.

☞ WHAT HE WANTS

- To protect his son.
- To assert himself.
- To give vent to his feelings of anger and hurt.
- To punish Jane. Note his attempts to 'guilt-trip' her.
- To find out if there is somebody else.
- To have his wife back.

☞ KEYWORDS brought thought done lost fault bothered stupid

Mark

" Have I brought Joe? Is that what you said? […] Have I brought Joe? […] Is that what you thought I'd do? Bring him halfway round the world to see some woman who might not even be his mother? […] Make him take malaria pills? Make him sit on a plane for hours and hours? No, I haven't brought him. Funnily enough. He's with my mum. He's been with my mum a lot lately. Do you know how old my mum is? She's sixty-five years old. She shouldn't be looking after a five-year-old: taking him to school, collecting him from school, giving him his tea. She shouldn't be putting him to bed, bathing him, bathing him while dad gets left with a TV dinner!

Pause.

Well? Aren't you going to say something?

Pause.

What, that's it is it? You're just going to stand there? Have you any idea what you've done to us? What you've done to Joe? […]

He's lost his mum, hasn't he? He doesn't understand any of this. He thinks it's his fault. And what am I supposed to say? Because I don't understand it either. Well?

Pause.

I don't believe this.

Pause.

What's going on, Jane?

Pause.

What's going on? […]

I've had it with this. I've really had it with this. I tell you, I'd rather have found you dead, I'd rather be identifying your body in some morgue, in some mortuary than have you standing there like this. Just standing there like nothing's happened. Are you seeing someone else? […]

Him is it? Jungle-book boy? […]

Are you pregnant? Is that what this is? […]

Were you pregnant? Because that's what she thought. She didn't say it but she thought it. You were pregnant and you had an abortion. […] Because if you did that, if you got rid of our baby because you can't be bothered to bring up another kid… […] That would have been a brother or sister for Joe… […] Well, what's this about a baby then? A baby in a bag? (*He points to the carrier bag.*) What's that then? […]

Well? […] Don't? Don't? Don't what? Don't what? You stupid, stupid, selfish cow! **"**

Mustafa

Naylah Ahmed

☞ **WHO**   Mustafa, thirties, British Asian, of Pakistani heritage.

☞ **TO WHOM**   Len, a senior police officer.

☞ **WHERE**   The recreation room of a UK prison.

☞ **WHEN**   Present day.

☞ **WHAT HAS JUST HAPPENED**   Mustafa is a devout Muslim. He is serving a prison sentence for the manslaughter of a teenage boy who died during an exorcism. Mustafa has been put in solitary confinement following a series of mysterious and violent incidents. Strange things happen around him. People are apt to behave more aggressively as if possessed; lights flicker on and off. His own personal prison officer, Len, quite out of character, has physically harmed him. He is known throughout the prison as Magic Mustafa and is regarded with deep suspicion. Mustafa, who is refusing to eat, to leave his cell and to take part in regulation activities, has been denied certain 'privileges'. He has had his prayer mat and notebook confiscated. Mustafa decides that one simple way of getting them back is to go to the recreation room. While the other inmates are watching a football match on television, Mustafa plays a round of pool with himself. It is enough to 'show willing', and Len agrees to return the items. He wants to know, however, why Mustafa is refusing to eat. Len points out that it is not Ramadan. In the speech that follows Mustafa explains why he is fasting.

☞ **WHAT TO CONSIDER**

- Mustafa has always protested his innocence.

- The 'djinn' or evil spirit that he maintains killed the boy is still present.

- Outside, in his community, opinion is divided. Some believe Mustafa a hero for having saved the boy from the djinn, others think him 'a crazed Mullah', who murdered a boy who, most probably, was suffering from some kind of psychosis. Read the play to find out more.

- To make meaningful contact with Len. Note how it is the first time in the play that he has spoken so freely and so copiously.

- To educate Len.

- (And more subliminally) to reassure Len that he, Mustafa, understands why Len was violent towards him and to show that he forgives him.

☞ KEYWORDS   storm   boiling   growling   rage   angry hungry   embarrassed   ashamed

Mustafa

❝ You know, I hated fasting when I was a kid. Didn't get it. Why would anyone think it'd be good for you to not eat or drink…? Even cheated sometimes. […] Once when I was older, it's Ramzaan and I'm in a shop trying to buy dates and get home to break fast with my brother and this old guy's with his grandson and he's holding up the queue. First he wants a few more items, then he's lost his wallet, then he remembers something else he needs – and he doesn't speak a word of English. He's Bengali, going on in his own language and the kid on the till, Pakistani kid, is too embarrassed to try and communicate with the old guy. So I storm to the front of the queue and I start yelling at the old guy and shouting at the kid on the till. I've been waiting ages, it's boiling hot and there's like a massive hole in my stomach growling for food, for water, for this old guy to get out of the way! I've got to get home, I'm telling them, to break fast! […] Kid behind the till just gets more embarrassed, takes my money, hands me the dates and I leave. Got home, too late despite my efforts. My aunt's yelling about me getting the wrong kinda dates, my brother's nowhere to be seen so I leave – still haven't eaten anything. I'm walking down the road in a rage, hungry as hell, and I see the old

Bengali guy sitting on the street with his grandson. They obviously didn't get out of the shop too soon so they're breaking their fast right there in the street. The kid's smiling and the old guy's feeding him a banana and an apple – they didn't have much. I see this tired old Bengali guy, in the boiling heat after a fifteen-hour fast, sipping water patiently, while his grandson eats the only thing they've got before they walk home. The kid's too young to fast – was eating chocolate in the shop but still he's munching away at the fruit – asking his gramps for more water. He sees me and… I'm ashamed – don't know why. So I look away, think I'm gonna cross over the road, keep walking. But the kid runs up and pulls me over – the old guy's telling me to sit. And he gives me a date, and a sip of water – pats me on the back, like he knows how angry and hungry I am. He offers me the fruit… Three of us sat there, on a pavement in the middle of the city sharing an apple, a banana and handful of dates. I haven't missed a fast since that day.

[…]

Thing is, Len, everyone in that queue – Granddad included – was fasting. All of us were hungry. Everyone was boiling. I'd been fasting for years and I never thought about that – ridiculous, I know. My brother, who I rushed home for? Wasn't fasting, out with his college mates somewhere in the city centre. That was it then. I wanted to know how an old guy like that, who must have been more knackered and hungry than me when I was shouting into his face in the shop – could smile and offer me a fair share at his meal when he had every right to kick off. Sometimes you have to do things for someone else – when you know you're going to get nothing back but trouble. Just cos it's the right thing to do… It ain't just about the food and drink, Len, it's about who we are, from sunup to sundown. Who we want to be… 99

Mydidae
Jack Thorne

☞ **WHO**   David, his age is unspecified, but we assume mid-twenties to early thirties. His father was the victim of racism. It is best, therefore, if David is played by an actor who looks as though his father could be other than white British.

☞ **TO WHOM**   His partner, Marian, a similar age.

☞ **WHERE**   In the bath.

☞ **WHEN**   Present day.

☞ **WHAT HAS JUST HAPPENED**   Taking place during the course of one day and set solely in the bathroom, the play tells the story of David and Marian. At first it appears an ordinary morning as we watch the couple perform their usual ablutions. He is shaving in readiness for an important pitch at work; she has a pee and then later shaves her legs. However, when she says to him, 'We just need to get through today' and he adds, 'I shouldn't be going in today, should I?' we sense something is wrong. Then, as David is alone in the bathroom getting ready, he inadvertently finds some contraceptive medicine in the bathroom cabinet. We are given to assume that this is another clue to the complexity of their troubled relationship. It is not until the evening, however, that we find out what is wrong. As the couple share a bath together Marian wants to know when was the first time David had his heart broken. What starts out as a sharing of information 'game' (she tells him about her first love, Pistol Pete, he tells her about university girlfriend Rachel Annes) soon becomes a bitter argument as he demands to know why she is taking birth control when they had agreed that they would try for a baby. It is at this point that we understand today is the anniversary of the death of their daughter and that Marian does not feel ready to replace her. She is angry at David and asks him, 'When was the last time you went to her grave? I had to go with my fucking mother.' He accuses her of lying to him by letting him live in hope. She then retorts, 'No, I let you fuck me. You did all the hoping by yourself.'

He is momentarily stunned into silence before he delivers the following speech.

☞ WHAT TO CONSIDER

- Marian went to a public school. David did not. In certain ways he feels inferior. He tells her, 'I'm not as clever as you. Well educated.'

- The pitch at work was unsuccessful. To what extent does David feel emasculated both professionally and personally?

- Later in the scene David tries to drown her.

- The feeling of helplessness he experiences at his loss of control.

- The anguish that he too feels at the death of their child.

- His inability to express his grief.

☞ WHAT HE WANTS

- To confess to something very personal.

- To prove that he too has suffered and can feel pain.

- To relive another episode which broke his heart and made him feel hopeless and inadequate.

☞ KEYWORDS   big/bigger   mattered   shit   willing   elegance
broke   heart

David

 Okay. Here's something that you…

Pause.

Okay. Here's information…

Pause.

When I was at school – I got picked for my – can't have been more than twelve – got picked for my school's football team. Right-back.

It was a big moment for me.

Even bigger one for my dad. Because – um – because he was my dad and that's what they… He always said the reason why he didn't play football professionally was racism, he went for a few trials – he was shit.

The reason why he didn't play football professionally was – he was shit. But anyway, me being picked for my school football team. That mattered.

I was pretty shit too.

But I was willing and would run around a lot. And that's pretty much all you need to be a right-back. […]

Anyway, I arranged to meet my friend Tony before the game. We said we were going to warm up together. He was making his debut too.

We went to the chip shop and bought a packet of chips which we shared. I remember it quite clearly. He put too much salt on the chips.

They tasted like shit.

Tony was a midfielder. Quite good. Sort of a midfield marauder but with a bit of elegance. Sort of Paul Ince-like. […]

Anyway, after about five minutes, these girls came over and started talking and, uh… We talked back. And then they left.

And then a couple of older lads with their own car – came over and gave us a couple of cigarettes… […]

And they said, we've heard about this thing – there's this old car up the rec and some kids are going to set fire to it you want to come watch?

We were due at school in about five minutes but Tony said 'yeah'. Immediately he said 'yeah'. And I said nothing. We drove up there. There wasn't anything on fire. The older boys said 'fuck it, that's annoying' and we said 'yeah'.

They didn't offer us a lift back. So we missed the football.

My dad asked afterwards whether I'd been ill. He was working nights at the time – couldn't get a better job – he took the night off to watch me play. I never made the team again.

Tony did.

Actually, Tony was eventually made captain.

You want to know when I first had my heart broke? Then. I was... I broke my own heart. That's what – that's what. I broke my own heart. **99**

NSFW

Lucy Kirkwood

☞ **WHO**   Sam, twenty-four, 'a working-class, university-educated boy from outside of London who now lives in Archway'.

☞ **TO WHOM**   Miranda, middle-aged editor of *Electra* magazine.

☞ **WHERE**   Miranda's office.

☞ **WHEN**   Present day.

☞ **WHAT HAS JUST HAPPENED**   Sam is an aspiring journalist. At the start of the play he is working for a men's magazine called *Doghouse*. One of his tasks has been to choose the winner of *Doghouse*'s 'Local Lovely' competition. But when it transpires that 'Carrie, eighteen, likes *Twilight* books and theme parks' is actually only fourteen and has not given consent for her picture to be used, Sam is forced to take the rap and loses his job. Here, nine months later, having split up from his girlfriend and desperate for work, he is being interviewed by Miranda for a position at women's magazine *Electra*. As a test of Sam's suitability, she has shown him photographs of famous female celebrities and has asked him to draw red circles on what he considers to be the flaws on their bodies. She also wants him to reveal what it was about his own girlfriend that he found repulsive. The speech that follows is his response.

☞ **WHAT TO CONSIDER**

- The objectification of women is equally noxious in the women's magazine as it is in the men's.

- Sam is sensitive and kind. He does not make judgements about people according to the way they look.

- He was and still is very much in love with Rona, who is six years his senior.

- He is dedicated and hardworking. He says he spent his teenage years largely revising.

- The present work climate, in which talented graduates are forced to take jobs as unpaid interns and for which they are overqualified.

- NSFW stands for 'not safe for work' and refers to the kind of material you would not want to be seen browsing in public.

☞ WHAT HE WANTS

- To feel connected.
- To feel complete.
- To be back with Rona.

☞ KEYWORDS love   gone   soulmate   funny   beautiful
brave   fearless   together   connected   shared   secret

Sam

❝ I can't think of anything. I'm sorry.

Beat.

I'd like to be able to but. I loved her. I do love her. I actually can't right now deal with the idea that she's gone, that I might not ever wake up with her again, or go on holiday, because I think, sorry if this is a bit, but I think she's my soulmate. Stupid things like I love watching her eat, the way she eats is so… and she's funny and beautiful and. Brave and – like, we were on the Tube once, it was really crushed and there was this man, he wasn't like a tramp, he was in a suit, he had a briefcase, and she realised this man had taken his, you know – his… penis, out, through his flies, and he was sort of, rubbing it on her but the Tube was so packed you know, so people didn't notice, but when she saw it, she started shouting really loud, 'Look at his chipolata!', till everyone was looking at them – and you'd think that would be really embarrassing, wouldn't you? But I just loved that, she's just, fearless and what happened is the whole Tube, together, starting chanting at him, we're all chanting together at this man, 'Chipolata! Chipolata!' and I thought: I actually feel like part of something, you know? For the first time in my life I feel like I'm part of something, like we, people, together, can change things. People can stand up and stop shit things happening. Because that's what it was like when I was with her, I felt… connected to the world, and all the things the world could be if we were just, better versions of ourselves, so it's like that better world was sort of a shared space that existed in both our heads, so there was like a world, that we lived in together, that we'd helped to make and it was just for us, it was our secret. We had a secret and we lived in it together and –

– and that's it, really.

I just really –

– love her. **99**

The Pain and the Itch

Bruce Norris

☞ **WHO** Cash, a successful plastic surgeon, American. His age is unspecified, but we assume mid-thirties.

☞ **TO WHOM** Mr Hadid, a cab driver.

☞ **WHERE** The living room in the home of Cash's brother Clay and his wife Kelly.

☞ **WHEN** Winter (around the time the play was written and first produced 2004–05).

☞ **WHAT HAS JUST HAPPENED** The play moves forwards and backwards in time as it recounts the events of Cash's family's Thanksgiving dinner and its disastrous consequences on the family of Mr Hadid. Mr Hadid and his wife have come to America to make a better life for themselves. Mrs Hadid speaks no English. She has been working for Cash's mother Carol as a cleaner and for Cash's brother Clay as a childminder. Then one day Mrs Hadid helps herself to half of Carol's expensive fig and nut loaf. It reminds her of the bread they eat back home. She does not have the English to explain this to Carol, and when Carol spots the bread in Mrs Hadid's handbag she assumes Mrs Hadid is a thief. Then when Clay's daughter develops a particularly nasty rash in her genital area the family assume it is something to do with Mrs Hadid. The police are alerted and go to Mr Hadid's house where they arrest her. Mrs Hadid is a diabetic and has just injected herself with insulin. Mr Hadid tries to explain to the police that it is vital his wife has something to eat, but they fail to take notice and Mrs Hadid goes into a coma and dies while in police custody. It is some time later that Mr Hadid is invited to Clay and Kelly's house. It becomes apparent that he intends to sue the family for wrongful accusation. We, meanwhile, come to discover that the cause of the daughter's itch is a venereal condition passed from mother to child and contracted when Kelly was having an affair with Cash. While they try to placate Mr Hadid and to persuade him not to take legal action, Cash does his best in the speech that follows to explain just how shallow their lives are. Shortly afterwards he adds: 'Look, you want to be more like us… (*Laughs.*) But we're a bunch of assholes.'

☞ WHAT TO CONSIDER

- Cash is perpetually fighting with his brother Clay. They are rivalrous. Cash slept with Clay's wife while she was pregnant.

- Cash has a partner, Kalina, a twenty-three-year-old Eastern European. The relationship is volatile.

- Cash's manner is brash and, to some, offensive.

- Read the play to understand fully the way in which the playwright examines the hypocrisies at the heart of American liberalism.

☞ WHAT HE WANTS

- To reveal to Mr Hadid both the superficiality and flimsiness of holding onto 'beliefs' in a world dominated by greed and gain, and the pointlessness of chasing the 'American Dream'.

- Decide to what extent that he too wants to dissuade Mr Hadid from filing a suit and that this is his way of going about it.

☞ KEYWORDS   believe/belief/beliefs   superficial   deeper serious

Cash

❝ So okay. So listen to this. So the other day this woman comes in my office. Says, to me, I think I want to get a nose job. […] (She) says, Doc, I want to get a nose job. The problem is – and get this, she says to me – the problem is, I don't believe in plastic surgery. I say, wait a second. I'm sorry, what? She says, not *believe like it doesn't exist*, it's that my belief system tells me not to agree with it. So I say, okay, which belief system is this? She says it's my personal belief. I think it's wrong. I don't think our lives should be determined by something so random as biology. I think that people should stop being hung up on the superficial. I have a wonderful personality. I'm a good friend. I'm funny. I'm lively. And still I don't have a boyfriend and I don't get the jobs I want. I'm at this enormous disadvantage all because I've got this nose. She says the world should not be that way. And that is what I believe. I believe it. And she says, so what can you say to me to put my mind at ease about the whole procedure? (*He thinks.*) Now, I'm trying to wrap my head around this. I'm trying to get this. I really am. I'm the doctor. Obviously I can't just act like... So I look at her. I put on a serious expression. And I say, well, let me ask you this: Which do you think came first, your *beliefs*, or your nose? Because maybe, and I could be wrong, correct me if I am, but *maybe* if you hadn't been born with this giant... *with* this nose, you wouldn't have developed these beliefs. She says, yes, but my beliefs go deeper. My beliefs are who I really *am*. And I say, yes, right, understood, but see, the problem is, I can't *see* your beliefs. Whereas your *nose*, to put it mildly, is readily apparent. And she says, you're acting like my beliefs aren't serious. And I say, as gently as I can, I say, well, perhaps not serious *enough* since you're already here for the nose job. And she says, I don't care for your attitude and I say okay. So she storms out. Goes to a friend of mine. He fixed her nose last week. Chin implant, too. My point is... well, you see what my point is. **"**

The People Next Door

Henry Adam

☞ **WHO**   Nigel Brunswick, English of 'mixed indeterminate race', 'the wrong side of twenty-five'.

☞ **TO WHOM**   Phil, a corrupt police officer.

☞ **WHERE**   Nigel's flat.

☞ **WHEN**   Not long after September 11th 2001.

☞ **WHAT HAS JUST HAPPENED**   Nigel lives on his own in a small housing association flat. He has a history of mental health problems and likes to smoke Class A drugs. He is unexpectedly visited by a police officer, Phil, who is on the hunt for Karim, Nigel's half-brother. Karim is an internationally wanted Muslim terrorist. He is on the run, and Phil believes it is just a matter of time before Karim will make contact with Nigel. As soon as Karim does so, Phil wants Nigel to tell him. Noticing that Nigel has been smoking Class A drugs in the flat, he threatens to arrest Nigel if he fails to cooperate. On this, their second meeting, Phil gives Nigel a stash of heroin in order to lure him further into helping with his undercover operation. He is physically rough with Nigel and tries to intimidate him. Nigel is insistent, however, that he has not seen Karim, but Phil keeps pressing him: 'He's your brother, though, isn't he?' The speech that follows is Nigel's response.

☞ **WHAT TO CONSIDER**

- Nigel is lonely and vulnerable. He has had psychotic episodes. His mother has disowned him and he hates his father.

- He is highly individual. You can be bold in your characterisation.

- Nigel's feelings about being mixed race. While he may have struggled with it as a boy, he comes to embrace it as an adult. He prefers to be called 'black' than 'brown', suggesting he sees race as a very political issue.

- The political background and the paranoia that surfaced in the wake of 9/11. In certain spheres, all Asian men were considered with suspicion.

☞ WHAT HE WANTS

- For Phil to leave him alone.

- To disassociate himself from Karim.

- To portray Karim as a polite and well-behaved child. In his first meeting with Phil, Nigel is adamant that Karim is a good boy and an unlikely terrorist.

- To give vent to his boyhood feelings of anger and confusion. Make a decision about whether Nigel has shared this story with anyone else before.

☞ KEYWORDS   brother   Paki   striking   shadow   posh related   Papa   baby-mothers   Mac   silence   tart   truth

Nigel

❝ Yeah, he's my brother, but we ain't close. Ain't like we grew up together or nothing. Ain't like I's going round his house every Christmas singing 'Silent Night'. Shit, I didn't even know the cunt existed till I was fourteen. I'm coming out of school one day, right, and I see this little Paki kid waiting there. He's looking at me, see, but I don't think nothing of it. People often look at me, you know? I got striking features or something. Anyway, after that, everywhere I go I see him, man. This Paki kid. He's like my fucking shadow man. My little Paki shadow. I walk, he walk. I stop, he stop. Eventually I just stop and fucking stare at him see, like this, see – (NIGEL *shows* PHIL *his best stern stare*.) and I'm like 'Okay Shorty, spill.' He's got this little posh voice man, and he's like – 'I know you, you're Nigel aren't you?' And I'm like – 'Hey, I know who the fuck I am. Who the fuck are you?' And he goes – 'My name is Karim. I think we might be related.' And I go – 'Yeah?' An he go – 'Yeah. I think you're my brother, Nigel.' And I'm like – 'Go away, kid, I don't have no brother,' but he just stands there right, this sweet little kid, and he go – and listen to this – he go 'Neither do I, but I think you might be him.' (NIGEL *raises an eyebrow to suggest this is the wisest, most profound sentence he has ever heard in his life*.) Neither do I, but I think you might be him. (*He waits for* PHIL *to see the wonder of this, but* PHIL *hasn't been smoking smack*.) He heard his uncles talking see. Laughing at his old man. Keep going on about 'Papa's little white boy'. That what they call him. Papa. Like he the big daddy or something – baby-mothers all over the shop. Like he some kind of Mac. (NIGEL *makes contemptuous sound with his saliva*.) [...] He resourceful. He a smart kid. Anyway – I'm like fuck off kid, I ain't your brother. I ain't no Paki, am I? But then I tell my mother. And I know from her face, man. I know from her silence. I know from her little tart eyes man. That kid telling the truth. It's like when I was little and I'd be going to school an people would be shouting– Paki, hey Paki – Paki, Paki, Paki, and I'm looking but I don't see no Paki. And they're shouting at me see, and I'm like – I'm fucking English man, I ain't no Paki. But they was right man, they was right. They know me better than I know myself. Paki. Nigel the Paki. (*Again the contemptuous sound*.) 🙿

Peribanez

Lope de Vega, in a version by Tanya Ronder

☞ **WHO**   Peribanez, a young Spanish farmer. You may like to use a regional accent in your depiction of him.

☞ **TO WHOM**   Casilda, his wife.

☞ **WHERE**   Peribanez's house.

☞ **WHEN**   Unspecified. The original play was written in the seventeenth century. In this version, which premiered at the Young Vic in 2003, the story was transposed to the twentieth century.

☞ **WHAT HAS JUST HAPPENED**   The monologue comes close to the start of the play. Peribanez and his new bride Casilda have made their way back from the church to Peribanez's house, accompanied by a small wedding party. As the couple are congratulated and the celebrations begin, Casilda says to Peribanez, 'You can't be as proud as I am to have you. If love was gold, husband, you'd be rich as a king.' The speech that follows is his response.

☞ **WHAT TO CONSIDER**

- Strictly speaking, the speech is from a classical text. If you are looking for a speech that is both heightened and contemporary, this would be an excellent choice.

- His way of describing Casilda is to compare her with things in the natural world – olives, a meadow, flowers, an apple, etc. Try to see, feel or smell these things in your imagination as you speak.

- Ocana is a town in central Spain in the province of Toledo.

☞ **WHAT HE WANTS**

- To declare his undying love for Casilda and to show that it is infinite.

- To idolise her.

- To bask in her reflected glory.
- To show her off.
- To offer/promise her all that he can.

☞ **KEYWORDS** love   heart   entire   beautiful   perfect
treasure   complete   worthy   Peasant   King   Queen
happiness   Devil's   Luck   Heaven

Peribanez

❝ You can't outweigh my love Casilda. My mouth will speak my heart and meet you anywhere, everywhere. I'd take the whole of Ocana and lay it at your feet. The entire town and every bit of land, field after field till the river's washed through all Portugal and disappeared into the Spanish sea.

What could be more beautiful than you? I can't think of anything. A grove of olive trees, heaving with olives, curling down with fruit? A meadow in early May, first light, when tiny flowers burst open, seeing the world for the first time? Or an apple – shiny and ripe? Thick golden oil, rich and clean in its clay pot? Everything pales, Casilda, next to you. I smell your lips, I can't imagine a better smell. Not even a wine that's been asleep in a tall dark cellar – white, crisp, perfect to drink. I'd compare you to roses if I were a gentleman, but I'm a worker and wine's the thing – but nowhere near as good as you. Could mushroom picking in December, the rain in spring, the miracle of wheat in August or October's grape juice come near to the treasure I'll have in my house? Who cares if the summer roasts me or the winter numbs me? I'm complete. I just have to look after this – (*Indicates his chest.*) it's your home – it needs to be worthy of you.

D'you think a Peasant can become a King through the peace in his heart? I think yes. Which means you're a Queen, Casilda. My Queen.

I want to bring you such happiness. Everybody'll wonder how did it happen? How did perfect Casilda turn out to have the Devil's own Luck? That's how happy Heaven will make you, wife, if I have anything to do with it. 𝟗𝟗

Pieces

Hywel John

☞ **WHO**   Jack, a pre-adolescent child.

☞ **TO WHOM**   Sophie, his godmother.

☞ **WHERE**   The sitting room of a large family house on the edge of a forest.

☞ **WHEN**   Present day.

☞ **WHAT HAS JUST HAPPENED**   Jack and his twin sister Bea have lost their parents in a car accident. The only person who is able to look after them is Sophie, their godmother. Sophie has not seen them in years, and Jack cannot remember her. The play starts straight after the funeral. Sophie, now their guardian, has come to stay in their large house on the edge of the forest. The three of them are in shock and are struggling to come to terms with what has just happened. On their second day together, Sophie is horrified to see the twins kissing. She is angry and tells them off. Upset, they disappear into the woods where they are gone for two hours. Sophie is distraught and telephones the police. While she is still on the phone, the twins return home. Bea has gone upstairs, and Jack tells Sophie about the woods.

☞ **WHAT TO CONSIDER**

- Jack is grieving the sudden loss of his parents.

- He is one of a twin.

- His relationship with his sister is strange and intense.

- Although they are children, both Jack and Bea are highly articulate and very direct. They like to dress as adults and mimic their parents' behaviour.

- Like many twins, there is something self-sufficient about Jack and Bea that others find unnerving. Decide to what extent growing up in such a remote place has compounded this.

- The constant power struggle between Sophie and the twins.

- Read the play to find out why Sophie has been absent from the family for so long and to discover what happens when the twins prepare a 'surprise' birthday party for themselves.

☞ WHAT HE WANTS

- To imagine his parents are still alive. Note the use of the present tense even though he is describing past events.

- To assert himself. In the previous scene, Sophie was telling him off. Decide to what extent Jack actively seeks to unsettle Sophie.

- To please Bea. She has asked Jack to explain to Sophie why they were kissing and what they were doing in the woods.

☞ KEYWORDS   fire   burst   surprise   kiss

Jack

❝ If Mum and Dad go for one of their long walks in the woods I get worried, even though they tell us where they've gone. I get a panic in my belly that builds up until it's like a fire and I almost can't bear it any longer. Didn't you feel that? […] Sometimes we run and find them if they've been gone too long. Didn't you want to run and find us? […] Are you scared? […] Of going in the woods. Don't you play in the woods? […] Didn't you ever walk in them with Mum and Dad? […] I know them really well. Mum, Bea and me build things in them, like traps and hiding places and stuff. […] When we run in to find them, when they've been gone a really long time, sometimes we find them just walking together and talking together and we find them because we can hear their voices through the trees. We sneak up on them and surprise them. Even though I have that panicky fire in my belly, I never call out their names to them. That's funny isn't it? I don't know why I don't call out their names, because in my belly I think maybe they've gone away for ever. I think it's because I know they're in those woods somewhere. We always find them somehow. […] One time we went running to find them and we couldn't hear them talking at all and it felt like the fire was going to burst out of my mouth or something. And the moment that I was going to shout out 'Dad and Mum!' I thought I heard Mum singing. Or I thought it was singing. But then it stopped really quickly. It was confusing. Then I heard it again – [...]

Like this:

(*Softly.*) 'Aaaaaahh.'

'Aaaaaahh.'

And we stopped dead still, because I knew it was Mum. For sure. And then she did it another time, but the note was a bit higher and by then I knew exactly where it was coming from. Then I think I heard Dad say Mum's name quite loudly. Then it was all quiet. And then Bea did the funniest thing: she sang it too.

'Aaaaaahh.'

I told her to shush, but Dad must have heard her because he shouted out our names and I was really annoyed for a moment, because I wanted to surprise them, and now we couldn't.

So we ran to where the singing came from, and we found them lying on the grass together beneath a big tree that Dad, Bea and me climb up sometimes. They were just lying on the grass, looking like they'd been running up a hill or something, all red-faced and smiling. I asked them that: 'Have you been running up a hill or something?' But Dad just laughed, and I don't know why, but he just laughed. Not at me, just like it was really funny that I asked it. Oh, it's because obviously there aren't any hills close by. I admit it: it was a stupid thing to say. Mum got up and gave us both a kiss and we walked home for tea.

And that's what Bea and me were doing in the woods. **99**

Playing the Victim

The Presnyakov Brothers, translated by Sasha Dugdale

☞ **WHO**   Valya, thirty.

☞ **TO WHOM**   The audience (see note on 'Direct audience address' in the introduction).

☞ **WHERE**   A room in a flat, in a town in Russia.

☞ **WHEN**   Present day.

☞ **WHAT HAS JUST HAPPENED**   Valya, thirty, is still living with his parents. Having dropped out of university, he works for the police, playing the victim in crime reconstructions. He is lazy and hates having to do anything that he does not want to do. He has become a master of excuses, and when his mother asks him to buy bread he convinces her that the flat bread they like is most probably poisoned, putting her completely off the idea and saving himself the trouble of going to get it. In this speech, close to the beginning of the play, he explains his reasoning.

☞ **WHAT TO CONSIDER**

- The play is a farce.

- Valya is an eccentric. Read the play to understand the way he thinks and speaks.

- At certain points in the script, the playwrights refer to him not as 'Valya' but as 'VOICE'. What might this suggest?

- The cultural and political background. Familiarise yourself with modern Russian history. At its heart the play makes comment on the corrosive effects of living in fear.

☞ **WHAT HE WANTS**

- To share in some detail his mechanisms and strategies for coping with fear. Throughout the play, Valya appears quite lonely. Decide to what extent he regards the audience as his friend with whom he is safe to express himself and give voice to his fears.

- To make sense of his own behaviour. To understand it himself.
- To survive.

☞ **KEYWORDS**   out   never   lazy   deeper   fear   afraid
scared   scare   drowned   drowning   punishing/punished/punish

Valya

❝ I was always good at thinking up ways to get out of things.
From when I was a kid, I never did anything I didn't want to.
And not because I was lazy… That's not the reason, or at least
that's a reason, but there's something else deeper which makes
me lazy. I think it's fear. Sometimes I'm afraid just to go out in
the street. I'm afraid to go for bread, or take a walk. And then
comes the laziness… Maybe, if you could find out, you might
find that there's a reason for fear, as well… Still, I've stopped
being scared of everything that used to scare me because I can
think of ways to get out of everything. Even in school, in
junior school, when they started taking us to the swimming
pool and I was scared of water – my mum almost drowned
when she was young, that was before I was born, so it must be
that it carried through to me… I mean, her fear of drowning
was carried through to me, although she was a good swimmer
actually, and even after she almost drowned she didn't stop
swimming – but I can't stand water, deep rivers, seas… I
never go in – not even to my knees… I don't like crossing
bridges either. And in school, when they started taking us to
the swimming pool for PE, I just didn't take my swimming
trunks with me and they wouldn't let me into the swimming
pool, because according to the rules you couldn't go
swimming in the same pants you were wearing for hygiene
reasons, although I suppose you could have been walking
around in clean pants anyway… But they didn't take into
account that people could be walking around during the day in
clean pants. Or I suppose you could take swimming trunks,
but dirty ones, and give everyone a nasty little dose of
something. Anyway, I never took my trunks, I used to pretend

I'd forgotten. They told me off, but never gave me a detention and I pretended I really wanted to go swimming and I begged them to let me in in the pants I was wearing... But they didn't let me and they thought they were punishing me like that. By the way, if people think you're being punished as it is, they never punish you any more... Yeah... **99**

Port Authority

Conor McPherson

☞ **WHO**   Kevin, 'maybe twenty', Dubliner.

☞ **TO WHOM**   The audience (see note on 'Direct audience address' in the introduction).

☞ **WHERE**   The play is set in the theatre.

☞ **WHEN**   Around the time the play was premiered in 2001. Summer.

☞ **WHAT HAS JUST HAPPENED**   Kevin has moved out of home to share a house with three others – his friend Davy, Davy's friend Speedy and Clare, the only girl.

☞ **WHAT TO CONSIDER**

- The play is a series of interwoven monologues charting the loves and losses of three generations of Dublin men.

- Kevin is unemployed and has no idea what it is that he wants to do with his life.

- He is something of a drifter and describes himself as the kind of person who would rather go with the flow than put up a fight.

- He is in love with Clare. Read the play to find out how their relationship develops.

- The significance of putting a plug on her CD player. Decide to what extent it might feel to Kevin that in that moment they are a couple. Later on in the play, Kevin enjoys the domesticity of going to the supermarket with Clare.

- When he talks about needing to get more organised, perhaps he is hoping that Clare will be the one to sort him out.

- Although Kevin is recounting events from the past, it might be useful to think of them as happening now. (Do not preempt what is going to happen. This will allow the story to feel more immediate.)

☞ WHAT HE WANTS

- For he and Clare to be together.

☞ KEYWORDS   special   sexy   weird   organised   useless
gorgeous   amber

☞ NB   This play offers a number of other speeches from
which to choose.

Kevin

❝ Clare was sticking luminous stars up on the wall and
ceiling of her room.

She wanted to paint the walls.

I said I didn't think we'd be let.

She said this was like a room where you sent your granny to
die.

Clare was very much sort of up to the minute.

When you saw her it took you a second but you knew she was
special.

She cared about her appearance but in a very discreet way.

She wore make-up but you couldn't see it.

She was definitely sexy but at the same time she was one of
the gang and very easy to be with.

For me anyway. And she saw me as like her mate.

Only when you saw her with a lot of other girls was she like…
a girl.

I was never one of those guys who hung around with a lot of
girls, as my friends.

If I knew a girl she was either the girlfriend of someone I
knew, or it was someone I was going out with.

So me and Clare was a weird thing for me.

So I was usually thinking about it a lot.

And wondering if… you know.

I was putting a plug on her CD player for her and I was looking through her CDs.

She told me to take a tape out of a box beside her bed. It was a demo tape. The guy she was seeing was in a band. […]

I stuck it in the machine and I was slightly pissed off because they actually sounded quite good.

They sounded like R.E.M. or someone.

'They're really good, aren't they?' Clare goes.

And I had to say yeah, they were.

They'd played support to some quite big bands like The Lemonheads and The Jesus and Mary Chain.

'We should get The Bangers to play with them some time,' I said.

Clare said yeah. But wasn't like a real yeah, more like… yeah! Bit too enthusiastic.

The Bangers were playing that night and we were going in to see them so I went into my room while Clare got ready.

I hadn't unpacked any of my gear. I was pulling all my clothes out but there was nowhere to put them, only on the chair.

So I put some trousers on the seat and and some tops on the back, and my trainers underneath.

And I stood back surveying this.

Thinking I had to get much more organised.

But who was I fooling. I was already useless.

Like I was starving and I'd no idea even if there was any food in the house.

I heard the shower go on and I could hear Clare going 'Oh my God!' at the state of the bathroom.

And later on we were down at the bus stop on the Malahide Road.

It was a gorgeous summer's evening.

All amber and a cool breeze.

Clare had one of her runners off shaking a little stone out of it.

I was leaning there looking at the mountains.

And Clare said up to me, she was kneeling on the ground, 'Are you alright?'

And I was looking at the mountains and nodding.

But I didn't think she could see me, so I said, 'Yeah, I'm fine.' **99**

Precious Little Talent

Ella Hickson

☞ **WHO**   Sam, nineteen, American.

☞ **TO WHOM**   The audience (see note on 'Direct audience address' in the introduction), and Joey, twenty-three, middle class, English.

☞ **WHERE**   A rooftop, New York City.

☞ **WHEN**   Christmas Eve, 2008.

☞ **WHAT HAS JUST HAPPENED**   The speech that follows comes at the very start of the play. It is intercut with passages of dialogue between Sam and Joey.

☞ **WHAT TO CONSIDER**

- Sam works as a carer for Joey's father George. George lives in an apartment beneath the rooftop. Joey has just arrived from London. She has not seen her father in two years and has no idea that he is suffering from dementia. At this point in the play, Sam does not realise that Joey is George's daughter.

- Sam's ambition is to be a doctor.

- He moved to New York when he was sixteen. Every night he would repeat to himself: 'If you're going to make your way in the world, it's going to take everything you've got.'

- He says he believes in 'God, my country, my family… Myself.'

- Sam's brand of optimism is typically American. Joey's cynicism is typically English.

- Within a month, Barack Obama will become America's first black president.

- Much of the play's discussion and humour resides in the differences between English and American sensibilities. Note how puzzled he is when she says, 'I don't believe in you.'

☞ **WHAT HE WANTS**

- To have sex with Joey.
- To fulfil a fantasy… 'like this is the moment that you might tell your kids that you met'.
- To live the American Dream.

☞ **KEYWORDS**   (*note how they come in pairs*) cruel and beautiful black and death   midnight, moonlit   tired and desperate   fast and quick (and furious)   smart stuff and slutty stuff

Sam

❝ (*To audience.*) It's Christmas Eve in the winter of two thousand eight and the night is cruel and beautiful and it feels like it's the first time it's ever been that way. I'm sitting on a rooftop, downtown New York City; in front of me midtown, pouring out into the night like a million luminous toothpicks, but right around me is black, black and death. I'm nineteen and I've got an erection, right tight into the front of my pants 'cos I can feel a woman's breath on the left side of my neck. This nervous little breath, panting, just beneath my ear; the moisture in it licking at me in the dark night and I so desperately want to turn around and suck that in, so desperately – but I keep my hands on my thighs, just like this and I say 'hey'.

[…] (*To* JOEY.) What's your name?

[…] No shit, mine too!

[…] No, it's Sam. I'm sorry – I don't know why I just said that.

(*To audience.*) She laughs this funny little laugh and it sounds funny so I say – You sound funny. […]

She says, all like that, all 'I'm English', like that. (*To* JOEY.) […] So… you're up here for, um – a little air? […]

(*To audience.*) So I'm thinking 'a little air', like taking a turn on the veranda, like a midnight, moonlit stroll, like Audrey

Hepburn at dawn before breakfast time at Tiffany's; like this is the moment you might tell your kids that you met and she says – […]

(*To* JOEY.) Hepburn? […]

How did you do that? […]

(*To audience.*) And then I'm sure you won't believe this, I'm sure you will have heard this said a thousand times before but piano music starts to play. […]

And suddenly we're running fast as our feet will take us, stamping down fire escapes, looking in on late-night offices where tired and desperate men are sitting and watching dollars dropping like flies but we're running, fast and quick and furious. We're headed down Bleecker where the lights are kind and the windows are crowded up with smart stuff and slutty stuff and it's cold, you see, so cold that my fingers get numb so as they might be tempted to let go of the very best thing that they have ever had the pleasure of holding on to –

(*To* JOEY.) You want to take the subway? […]

(*To audience.*) We take the uptown 6 train that goes all the way up and down Manhattan, scratching its back along the side of Central Park – we take it all the way up through Astor and Union and 59th and 96th and all the way on up to Harlem and when we get to the top we just come right back again and on our way back down we just can't stop looking at each other and we laugh and we put our hands over our faces like kids in a bathtub – […]

I take her hand and I lead her off that train and I've judged my timing right because we emerge right into the middle of Grand Central Station. […]

And do you know what I did – right then, right in the middle of Grand Central Station? I pulled her right around and I kissed her, real hard. And when I stopped, when I stopped and stood back and I looked at her, she said the strangest thing, she said… 'I don't believe in you.' **"**

The Pride

Alexi Kaye Campbell

☞ **WHO**   Oliver, mid-thirties, gay.

☞ **TO WHOM**   Philip, mid-thirties, his partner.

☞ **WHERE**   The sitting room of Oliver's flat.

☞ **WHEN**   2008.

☞ **WHAT HAS JUST HAPPENED**   The play tells the story of two sets of characters, both with the same names, from 1958 and from 2008. In 1958, Sylvia is unhappily married to Philip. He is gay but in denial. When he meets her friend and colleague Oliver, he is unable to control his feelings of attraction. But the practice of homosexuality is illegal, and their torrid affair ends unhappily. In 2008, Oliver and Philip, both friends of Sylvia's, have been a couple for a year and a half, but Oliver is promiscuous and Philip has ended their relationship and moved out. The speech that follows comes towards the end of the second scene in the play and is the first set in 2008. Oliver has employed the services of a male prostitute who is dressed in Nazi uniform. However, Oliver soon goes off the idea of having sex with the man, and they sit and talk instead. Oliver confesses that he is sad about his boyfriend leaving him. Philip then arrives back at the flat unexpectedly and is shocked to see the stranger. He had thought Oliver would be out and had come to pick up the last of his things. The man leaves, and Oliver tries unsuccessfully to pretend that he had met him at a fancy-dress party. Oliver tells Philip that he loves him and does not want him to leave. But Philip is depressed by Oliver's need to have sex with other men. Oliver tries to explain to Philip that having sex with strangers takes the form of an addiction and that he cannot help it. As he tries to justify his actions, he is reminded of a conversation he overheard when he was a teenage boy.

☞ **WHAT TO CONSIDER**

- Unlike his 1958 counterpart, Oliver is free to express and practise his homosexuality.

- To what extent does this increased freedom bring with it a different set of responsibilities and problems?
- Oliver is in turmoil. He genuinely loves Philip above all other men, but has no control over his sexual urges.

☞ WHAT HE WANTS

- To understand himself.
- To share this understanding with Philip so that Philip will forgive him.
- To prevent Philip from leaving.

☞ KEYWORDS   good   boy   lost   soul   weird   knowing

Oliver

❝ There's something I never told you. […] This thing that happened when I was young. Once, I must have been seventeen or something and I was staying at my aunt's. My mother's sister. The one you met. […] And this woman came by. A friend of hers. And I was on my way out. So my aunt introduced me to this woman and I said hi, how are you and all that and then ran out. But a minute later I realised I'd left something. My sweater or something. So I ran back in the house to get it and then I realised that the two women – my aunt and her friend – were talking about me. But they hadn't heard me come back in the house. And I stood there, rooted to the spot. And listened. I couldn't hear everything but then – then this thing happened. I heard my aunt saying something along the lines of, 'He's a good boy but a bit of a lost soul.' Actually, it wasn't along the lines of. It was her exact words. I heard them. 'He's a good boy but a bit of a lost soul.' And the weird thing is – the weirdest – was that even before she said it, I kind of knew what she was going to say, like I'd heard her speak the words before, like her saying it and me knowing what she was going to say was all kind of tied up. Happening at the same time. 'He's a good boy but a bit of a lost soul.' **❞**

Purgatorio

Ariel Dorfman

☞ **WHO**   Man.

☞ **TO WHOM**   Woman.

☞ **WHERE**   A white room, in Purgatory.

☞ **WHEN**   All time.

☞ **WHAT HAS JUST HAPPENED**   A Man and a Woman are alone in a white room. At first we assume they are in a mental asylum and that he is her analyst. We soon come to understand, however, that they are in Purgatory and that he is her interrogator. She has murdered her two sons and her husband's younger lover. Unless she can repent, she will remain in the room for ever. Then, as the lights go down and back up again, it is the Man who is being interrogated by the Woman. He has committed suicide following the murder of his two sons by his estranged wife. He desperately wants to leave the room, to be reborn into the afterlife, and is quick to repent of any wrongdoing. However, the Woman is not convinced and accuses him of fabricating mistakes in order that he can be fast-tracked out of there. She produces a vase which he claims to have broken and then blamed the accident on his grandmother, and for which he is now sorry. 'Except,' she says, 'there is nothing to be sorry for.' The Woman maintains that he is making it up. In a statement written by his grandmother, his grandmother states: 'I can't forgive myself for having let the child be punished for something I did.' The Man, however, is insistent that it was he who broke the vase. The speech that follows is his version of events.

☞ **WHAT TO CONSIDER**

- The play takes its inspiration from the Ancient Greek legend of Jason and Medea, in which Medea kills their children because of Jason's infidelity.

- At the heart of the play lie questions to do with retribution and forgiveness. You may like to read other plays of Ariel Dorfman, *Death and the Maiden*, *Reader* and *Widows*, in which these themes are further explored.

☞ WHAT HE WANTS

- To prove that he is sorry.
- To leave the room.
- To be reborn.
- To have 'another stab at life'.
- Redemption.

☞ KEYWORDS   hated   bothered   lunged   angrily   blamed
swore   shouted   stupid   dribbling   trembled   pity   sorry

Man

❝ We were at lunch, as usual. Alone, the two of us, my grandmother and me. I hated having to accompany her, hated my mother for forcing me to. Could you pass me that, pass me this, this that this that that. Just to bother me, to make me pay attention to the old woman. Till my grandmother asked me for one last thing, I can't remember what it… a napkin, maybe – […] Whatever it was, it was at her fingertips, all she had to do was move her finger an inch, less than an inch. I lunged across the table for it, angrily, no patience whatsoever, and broke the damn vase. And when my mother came in at the end of the meal, I blamed my grandmother. I swore she'd done it. And I liked it when my mother shouted at her, you stupid old woman. Stupid old woman. Years later I went into her room one last time, before I left on that journey – and crumbs were dribbling from her lips and her hand went out slowly, so slowly to the crumb and brought it to her mouth that trembled and it fell again and I tried to help her but she just stared past me as if I didn't exist and I saw she was going to die soon all by herself in that room and I felt a twinge of pity then, a hint of what I would feel later, now, when I think about her, that I never saw her again, never told her I was sorry. ❞

Purple Heart

Bruce Norris

☞ **WHO**   Purdy, twenties, an ex-Corporal, Vietnam veteran, American.

☞ **TO WHOM**   Carla, a soldier's widow.

☞ **WHERE**   The living room of Carla's home in a medium-sized city in the American Midwest.

☞ **WHEN**   Late October, 1972.

☞ **WHAT HAS JUST HAPPENED**   Carla's husband has been killed in Vietnam. She has become an alcoholic. She lives with her son, Thor, and mother-in-law, Grace. The play begins at 6 p.m. one evening, just before the family are about to eat. Shortly after the start of the play, Purdy arrives unexpectedly. Carla and Grace do not know him and assume that he was a friend of Carla's husband and that he has come to pay his respects. Purdy says to Carla, 'You don't remember me, do you?' and goes on to explain that they met in the military hospital where he was recovering, having lost his right hand in a landmine blast. She was in the same hospital being treated for shock, having blacked out following a visit to her dead husband's coffin. She explains to Purdy that she cannot remember having met him and confesses that she was hospitalised because she had drunk too much. In a long monologue, she reveals the truth about her husband's violent temper and the way in which he physically and emotionally abused her. She tells Purdy that, among his personal effects, she found a picture of her husband with a fourteen-year-old prostitute sitting on his lap and that it was hardly surprising that she went on a drinking binge. Purdy's speech comes in response to her outpouring.

☞ WHAT TO CONSIDER

- The social, political and historical context. Take time to research the Vietnam War and the political debate it fuelled in America at the time.

- At this point in the play, we assume that Purdy is an innocent victim of war. We will later discover that Purdy is not all that he seems. The 'landmine' story is questionable; he too, is a drinker, having lied about the fact; and in a dark twist to the story we come to understand that Purdy has raped Carla, while she was lying unconscious in the hospital. Carla has no memory of this and is now unknowingly pregnant by him.

- Read the play to understand fully his motives and darker intentions. Knowledge of the play as a whole will enable you to find the layers required when playing the speech. It appears that he has Carla's best interests at heart and that the story of the burning building is just a way to illustrate his point about not being judged or controlled. However, when you read on, the monologue takes on an altogether different and sinister meaning.

- You will need to explore the underlying threat in order to add weight and menace to his character. Watch that you do not overdo it, however: he keeps his secrets well!

- In the playtext, Carla has the line: 'They go back because the burning building is beautiful.' I have taken the liberty of giving it to Purdy as if he is repeating back what she has said to him, in order to complete the speech.

☞ WHAT HE WANTS

- To side with her. Not long after this speech, he says, 'What an astonishing volume of horseshit people expect you to swallow. Do you know what I mean?' and 'I'm trying to say that it might be a good idea for you not to blame yourself so much.'

- To gain her trust.

- To test her, by seeing how far he can go before she remembers. Note how he too, like the arsonist, has returned to view the 'damage'.

- To seduce her.

☞ **KEYWORDS**   negative   wrong   bad   selfish   greedy   conscience   soul   wickedness   mistake   love   perfect   beautiful   whip/whips

Purdy

66 May I make an observation? You seem to be the sort of person who has a lot of negative feelings about herself. You tend to feel like maybe you've done a lot of things wrong. Am I right about that? [...] I say this because until recently I had very negative thoughts about *myself*. I had begun to think that all of the things that I wanted, all of the things that I enjoyed must be bad and that I must be a bad person for wanting them. It's hard to say *exactly why* I felt this way. I don't know. I never had a lot of friends, and my father would tell me, with some frequency, that I *was* a bad person. That I was selfish and greedy and thought only of myself, not of the other person, that I didn't take the feelings of others into consideration, and that made *me* a bad person. And naturally I believed him because he was my father and why would your father tell you something that wasn't true? So I said to him how am I supposed to become a better person? How do I achieve that? And he said simply listen to your conscience. And I was confused. I said is my *conscience* the same as my *soul*? No, he said, your conscience is different. Your *conscience* is a little angel that sits right here on your shoulder and he tells you when you've done something bad. It's sitting there right now. It never goes to sleep and it never gets tired. I see. So I said what if you want to do something even though your conscience tells you not to? And he said that's what we call wickedness. But I said, what if the conscience makes a mistake? What if it takes over and it makes you feel bad about everything you love? Everything perfect or beautiful? And he said it never makes a mistake. *Never*, I said? He said think about this: he said why do you think people who set a building on fire always come back to the scene of the crime? Why else would they do that? They don't *want* to go to *jail*, do they? No, their conscience *makes* them come back. He said their conscience knows it was wrong, and it has a little tiny whip and it whips them and whips them until they go back to that burning building to see how wicked they were. And I thought about this for a few seconds. I really had to think. Because that didn't seem

right to me. So I thought about it very hard and after a few seconds I turned to him and I said – [They go back because the burning building is beautiful.] That's exactly what I said. I didn't get my allowance that week. **99**

Push Up

Roland Schimmelpfennig, translated by Maja Zade

☞ **WHO**   Robert, early thirties, young executive.

☞ **TO WHOM**   The audience (see note on 'Direct audience address' in the introduction).

☞ **WHERE**   His office in a large corporate building. The exact business of the company is unspecified.

☞ **WHEN**   Present day.

☞ **WHAT HAS JUST HAPPENED**   Set in a highly successful and competitive corporation, the play moves forwards and then backwards in time. In the speech that follows, Robert is continuing with a recollection from a previous speech, 'it was the best sex I've ever had', in which he describes his and Patrizia's first meeting. He describes how attracted they are and, without words, sneak off from the party their boss Kramer is throwing. At this point in the play, we, the audience, are privy to some of what happens next: Patrizia has been asked by her boss Kramer to get in touch with Robert about a new advertising campaign the company intends to launch. She has previously enjoyed huge success with an advertisement that she now wants to recreate in every detail; only this time, the setting will be New York's Central Park. Robert hates the idea, and the couple have a bitter argument about it. Both Robert and Patrizia, wrongly assuming that their moment of passion meant nothing more to the other than a fling, are hell-bent on destroying each other. The success or failure of this new advertising campaign becomes the focus of their intent. However, it is Kramer who gets the final say. Read the play to find out who 'wins'.

☞ WHAT TO CONSIDER

- The world of the play is cold and clinical. There is a buzz to be had from striking a deal or having sex with a near stranger, but it is a world without trust, loyalty or love.

- Robert is described as 'successful', 'a whiz kid', 'ambitious', enthusiastic', and everyone knows that 'the stuff that reaches Kramer goes past his desk first'.
- In Patrizia, he has met his match
- The style of the play. Intercut between their scenes, he and Patrizia have almost identical monologues.

☞ WHAT HE WANTS

- To prove his virility.
- To justify his handling of the situation.
- To have Patrizia.
- Revenge.

☞ KEYWORDS   dark   smells   kiss   sex   spectacular belonged   fling   angry   pay

☞ NB   This play offers a number of other speeches from which to choose.

Robert

❝ It's dark in Kramer's office. She's standing with her back towards me, by the window.

I'm right behind her. She smells just like I imagined. If Kramer walks in now and finds us in his office we'll both get fired. On the spot.

I put my hands round her waist and turn her. We kiss. I push her against the window and pull up her dress. We have sex. Incredible, passionate sex.

Pause.

Afterwards we go back to the party and mingle, and Kramer says: Robert, I was about to look for you –

Short pause.

Of course I was going to call her the next day. But –

Short pause.

– but then I didn't. I wanted to – but I didn't. Although in my job I often make the first move, I don't have a problem with that – in general. Either at work or –

Short pause.

– in my private life.

But – but this, this was different. This was something else. This was not just a fling. There was more at stake here. This was big.

This woman was important. This woman was spectacular –

Short pause.

You can't just call a woman like that. It would have been a mistake, I'm still certain of that. I didn't want her to think I needed to get in touch with her.

We were in the same league, we just worked in different areas: we were both competent, flexible, innovative and hard on ourselves and on others. Even now, in our early thirties, we had jobs others will never manage to get. She didn't have one up on me and I didn't have one up on her. She was like me: I was like her, and I wanted her to know that. We – her and me – we belonged together.

And that's why I couldn't call her.

Short pause.

But I tried to bump into her. In the car park or in the lobby by the lifts. Or in the canteen or in one of the little Italian restaurants round the corner. But I didn't find her. I looked for her, I tried to find out when she arrived for work in the morning and when she left, but it didn't work.

Short pause.

And she didn't call. She didn't get in touch. No phone call, no note. Maybe for her I was just a fling in her boss's office. She wasn't interested in me. She didn't get in touch. Maybe she thought I wasn't worth it.

She didn't give a damn about me.

Short pause.

Gradually I got angry. I got angry because she didn't call me.

Short pause.

I got angry because she didn't realise who she was dealing with, what we could have been together. I meant nothing to her, and she was going to pay for that. One day I was going to really make her pay for that.

Short pause.

Nonetheless I kept on looking for her: in the car park, in the lobby, in front of the lifts, and in the canteen and after work in the little restaurants and bars round the corner. And then Kramer came up to me and said it was time for a new ad. Had I ever met Patrizia – and that I should get in touch with her. It was bound to be interesting for both of us. **"**

The River

Jez Butterworth

☞ **WHO**   The Man, late thirties, but could be played younger.

☞ **TO WHOM**   The Other Woman.

☞ **WHERE**   A cabin on the cliffs above the river.

☞ **WHEN**   Present day.

☞ **WHAT HAS JUST HAPPENED**   The play tells the story of four unnamed characters. They are described only as 'The Man', 'The Woman', 'The Other Woman' and 'Another Woman'. In the first scene, The Man has invited his girlfriend, The Woman, back to his cabin. They plan to go fishing. The scene then fades to dark and then up again to reveal the man on the telephone reporting the woman missing. As he does so, there is the sound of a door banging, and a woman's voice is heard from off. He tells the police that she is back and that it was a false alarm. A woman enters, but it is Another Woman, who is played by a different actress. However, they talk as if she were the first. He asks her, 'Where were you?' and tells her that he has called the police. Later she exits to the bedroom. He prepares supper. The (first) Woman then enters, towelling her hair, again as if nothing had changed. After supper, The Man asks her to go and get something he found when he was fishing once. He does not say what but tells her that it is in the bedroom in a hatbox under the bed, wrapped in a green handkerchief. She goes but when she re-enters she is The Other Woman. This same switch happens twice more before The Other Woman asks, 'How many women have you brought here?' The speech that follows is The Man's response.

☞ **WHAT TO CONSIDER**

- The play is mysterious and haunting. The language lyrical.
- It begs many questions about the nature of love, lies and the truth.
- The Man is very physical and sensuous. He is obsessed with fishing and most of his imagery is from the natural world.

- At the very end of the play, a third woman (Another Woman) appears.

- Read the play to understand fully its twists and turns.

☞ WHAT HE WANTS

- To prove to The Other Woman that she is the one and only true love.

- To possess her.

☞ KEYWORDS   ghost   desperate   invisible   snare   sacred
imposters   lost   looking   lie

Man

❝ You really want to know? (*Pause.*) When I was about twelve my uncle said he'd brought lots and lots of women here. Fillies he called them. And he said how he used to do the same things with each of them. The same routine. He'd bring them here around sunset, pour them a large Scotch. Take them fishing then bring them back and quote have his wicked way. He said he'd brought dozens here. So many he said he'd get them mixed up. Have to write down their names. And he laughed. He laughed that big laugh of his. But he suddenly had the eyes of a ghost. And the mouth of some desperate creature caught in an invisible snare. As I went to sleep that night I promised myself I would only bring one woman here. The woman I wanted to spend my life with. The woman I wanted to be with for ever. She would come here, and it would be sacred. It would be something I had only shared with her and her alone.

[…]

Earlier this evening, when you came back. I said something to you. And you laughed it off. […]

It's okay. You were surprised. Not as surprised as me. Trust me, I didn't want to say it. But I had no choice. Because there was nothing else in my head or in my whole being. There was no way forward except through that. There was no next breath without it. And you're right. I may forget who you are. I may bring other women here, to this place, and I may tell them I love them, and make love to them. But they will be imposters. And I will be a ghost. Because it means I will have lost you. My body, my brain, my lungs, my stomach, my guts, legs, arms will be here but I won't be. I will be out there, looking for you. And if we meet somewhere, at a restaurant, or a party and I'm with someone, I want you to know that they are by my side only because you are not. And she will be beautiful. And I will be laughing and smiling and she will be laughing and smiling, but she will be laughing at a lie. Because all I will have done to that person is lie to them. All I will do to anyone else, forever, from this moment forward, anyone who isn't you, is lie. I have no choice. (*Beat.*) I have no choice. **99**

Snuff[*]

Davey Anderson

☞ **WHO**   Kevin, Glaswegian, his exact age is unspecified, but we assume early twenties.

☞ **TO WHOM**   Billy, his friend.

☞ **WHERE**   A small room in Kevin's high-rise flat in Glasgow.

☞ **WHEN**   Strictly speaking, around the time the play was first produced in April 2005. However, the speech is still applicable to the present day.

☞ **WHAT HAS JUST HAPPENED**   Kevin lives in a housing-scheme flat in a run-down Glasgow tower block. At the start of the play he is watching a video. It is an interview he has recorded with his sister Pamela. He is the interviewer. He is questioning her about where she got her new clothes from, and, as he becomes increasingly aggressive towards her, Pamela threatens to get him 'done over'. She says she will tell 'Billy' what he has done to her. Kevin retorts that Billy is not around and that he has been away for two years. At that moment there is a knock on the door. Kevin turns off the video and answers it. It is his old friend Billy, a soldier, back from Iraq. Billy asks where Pamela is, and Kevin tells him that Pamela's dead. Billy assumes that Kevin is joking. As the two men try to catch up, there is an awkwardness between them. They share some reminiscences, but it is clear that Kevin has become increasingly paranoid of the outside world. He has surrounded himself with piles of videos that he has taken. He tells Billy that it is a private project that he is working on. He takes a Polaroid picture of Billy and writes Billy's name on the back. He explains to Billy that he just needs one more subject and then the project is done. The speech follows directly after this.

☞ **WHAT TO CONSIDER**

- Both men are at war. Billy's was a real-life war. Kevin's is in his mind.

[*] Published in the volume *Scottish Shorts*

- Kevin feels abandoned.
- He feels invaded.
- The kind of poverty and paucity of expectation that prompts young men like Kevin to adopt racist views and to display violent behaviour.
- Read the play to discover how Billy becomes Kevin's last 'subject'.

☞ WHAT HE WANTS

- To give vent to his feelings of frustration. 'Naebody fucking telt me.'
- To find someone to blame.
- To shame Billy for not having been there.

☞ KEYWORDS   mad   mental   demolish   doom

Kevin

❝ Ye want tae know something, Billy? See since you left, this place has gone tae the dogs. Swear tae God. All the decent folk moved oot. Got transferred doon tae the new flats by the river. Most of the flats were empty. So they started boarding up all the windaes and the doors. The only people left were the junkies, the hardnuts, the perverts and the freaks. Turned intae a madhoose, this place. A big, damp, concrete, mental asylum.

The coonsil telt us they were gonnae level this block, ye know? Blow it up. They gave us six month. They says, as soon as we find ye somewhere else tae live, we're gonnae demolish the flats. So we waited. Nothing happened. Six month passed, still nothing. And I thought, well, this is it. They're jist gonnae demolish the flats, junkies and all. Bury us alive in a mountain of ash and rubble.

I wis quite looking forward tae it, tae be honest. Jist kind of resigned myself tae the fact, ye know? Jist got used the idea of inevitable doom.

Then wan morning this truck pulls up doonstair. These guys come oot and start unloading. Furniture. Fucking sofas and tables and beds and that. Loads of them. I wis like that, oh aye, whit's this all aboot? And they start taking all this stuff intae the empty flats. Opening the doors, fixing the windaes, getting them ready. I says tae wan of the guys, whit's gon on? He's like that, oh we're jist moving the furniture. I says, aye, but who's it for? I dinnae ken, that's nane of ma business, I jist get paid tae shift the furniture.

And see when they arrive, it's the middle of the night. These two coaches drive up tae the flats. I hear the engines. It wakes me up. I goes tae the windae, looks doon. I cannae see too well. The street light's flickering. But something fucking weird is going on. All these people are getting bundled aff the buses, wae carrier bags and that.

And they're all stauning there. And no a single wan ae them has a white face. I'm like that, fuck me.

I sprint doon the stair. The whole car park's swarming wae fucking foreigners. Where's the driver? Naebody's listening. Where's the fucking driver? Some of them look at me but naebody speaks. Fuck's sake, dae nane of yous cunts speak any fucking English?

Then they all start piling in the door. Up the lift and up the stairwell. Stopping off at every flaer tae fill up their new luxury apartments. I'm trying tae block the entrance, but there's too many of them.

Why the fuck does somebody else no wake up and see whit's going on?

If only Billy wis here, I thought, he would help me. He'd be doon here in a flash. We could take them on, jist the two of us. Dae a bit of kung fu and whip all of their black asses. We'd drive them oot before they could say Osama bin Laden. We'd fucking show them.

But you wurnae here. You were away. And it wis jist me. I couldnae stop them on ma ain.

Next thing ye know, all the doors slam shut, the buses drive off. Silence. I'm left stauning there in the pissing rain. Freezing my bollocks off. No a fucking thing I can dae aboot it. I shouts up at the flats, naebody telt me!

That's the worst of it. It all jist happened like that. Naebody fucking telt me. **99**

Stoopud Fucken Animals

Joel Horwood

☞ **WHO**   Charlie, twenty-two, from Leiston in Suffolk.

☞ **TO WHOM**   Belle, thirty-six, his mother, a prostitute.

☞ **WHERE**   A room in a brothel, King's Cross, London.

☞ **WHEN**   Present day. Autumn

☞ **WHAT HAS JUST HAPPENED**   Charlie and Dim are non-identical twins. They live in Leiston, a small Suffolk town close to Sizewell Nuclear Power Station. Charlie works for a company selling bull semen, and Dim is a paper boy. When Charlie discovers that his 'mother' Karen is not his mother but his grandmother, he goes to London to look for his real mother, Karen's daughter. He has the telephone number of a phone box in King's Cross and knows that her name is Annabelle. Annabelle (or 'Belle') has been working as a prostitute. Posing as a client, Charlie has booked a session with her. Charlie and Dim were born by caesarian section. Charlie has asked Belle to remove her clothing. She has a scar in the exact place a C-section would be. In the speech that follows, he attempts to get her to reveal her true identity.

☞ **WHAT TO CONSIDER**

- Charlie and Dim, whose real name is Horace, have been the butt of public taunts for as long as Charlie can remember.

- Charlie changes his name from Charlie Redhead to Charlie Bronson.

- The lack of opportunity for young men like Charlie and Dim.

- Charlie hates his job selling bull semen and quits it.

- Dim gets a job servicing the vending machines at the nuclear plant.

- Karen works in the local chip shop. She is drink dependent.

- Coincidentally, the boys come face to face with their real father 'Lefty'. Charlie is angry at him: 'He's fucken stumped me, Dim.'

- Lefty was twenty-six when he slept with Annabel.

- The Suffolk accent. If it is not already native to you, make a good study of it. It is quite different from the westcountry accent.

☞ WHAT HE WANTS

- A confession from Belle.

- To be reunited with his mother.

- His mother's love.

- To relieve his feelings of abandonment.

☞ KEYWORDS   story   funny   comedy   fairytale   scandal
cut   beat   wound   scar

Charlie

❝ I'm gonna… […]

I'm gonna sit for a minute. I've got a story for you… That's about two boys what thought their nan and grandad was their parents. Funny, in't it? The woman who said she was their mum, she was their grandmum, I mean it's a boney-fidey comedy. Their grandad fucked off, before they were born, couldn't handle it, I guess, thought his daughter was gonna be the next… next Torvill or Dean or whoever, she was the under-fourteens roller-skating champion of Suffolk, in the papers, everything but… she got up the duff. The grandmum pretended to be pregnant, pillow up her shirt, all of that fairytale crap. Thought it might save her daughter, see, back then that'd be worse than now, police, scandal, she'd lose her job, and it's small round there. People don't forget.

Beat.

They cut 'em out. The twins, second one hardly breathing, they said the first beat him up in the womb. He got breathing proper, but han't never got over it. The grandmum kicking up a stink in the little clinic of a place, middle of the night, drunk. They sew the girl up and the grandmum's there, cooing at the kids, whilst her daughter – their mother – she's off. Stitches and all. They reckon her walking woulda kept that wound open, stopped it from healing proper.

Pause.

Annabelle, her name was. I been watching the payphones round here for the last five days. There's only one what work anyway and I followed everyone what used it.

Beat.

She'd have a scar. **99**

Terminus

Mark O'Rowe

☞ **WHO**   'C' – Male, thirties, from Dublin.

☞ **TO WHOM**   The audience (see note on 'Direct audience address' in the introduction).

☞ **WHERE**   Unspecified. You may like to imagine you are in all the different locations as he describes them.

☞ **WHEN**   Present day. After dark.

☞ **WHAT HAS JUST HAPPENED**   The play is a series of three interconnected monologues, charting the events of one extraordinary night in and around Dublin. The speech forms the start of character C's story.

☞ **WHAT TO CONSIDER**

- The play is fantastical. What starts out as an ordinary evening soon becomes a tale of supernatural proportions.

- C has sold his soul to the Devil for the price of an exquisite singing voice. However, his acute shyness prevents him from singing in public, and what was intended to be the most powerful tool for seduction has left him with such a hatred of the world, and of women in particular, that he has become a serial killer.

- He goes to the disco with the sole purpose of picking up a woman he can fuck and then savagely murder.

- 'Gee' is a slang word for vagina.

- The use of rhyming words throughout the speech. Make space for these words to land. They are like the beat of music and should pulse through you, driving you on.

- The language. Poetic and muscular, the text is as heightened as its subject matter. You can be bold in your playing of it.

- His lack of a name. What might this suggest?

☞ WHAT HE WANTS

- To vent his rage.
- To have sex. Decide to what extent this is about craving power as much it is about seeking pleasure.
- To escape his loneliness.

☞ **KEYWORDS**   manoeuvre   meander   quell   craving unfussy   heinous

☞ **NB**   This play offers a number of other speeches from which to choose.

C

❝ I pop a Locket in my mouth, suck, then bite into the shell and – fucking hell! – the spill of honey? I *never* fail to find it yummy.

Putting the packet back in my pocket for later, I manoeuvre my body out of the motor, meander over and, as I enter, am shouldered aside by three wankers as they swagger past, and the last, thinking it's fucking gas, looks back and, like a roguish retard, laughs.

I pay at the counter and enter this community centre doubling as a disco. This copious Cashel congregation of middle-agers, country-livers, sundry lonely lovelorn fuckers looking for partners.

Though I remark there's plenty of younger stuff as well, and it's difficult enough to quell this desire to leer or stare, provoked by the barely legal bodies soaking, arses jolting, nipples poking, evoking so prevailing a craving, I'm quaking.

Control it, you fuck. Hold it in check lest you wreck any chance of a dance in the slow set, reserved as it is for the nervous, the cautious, such as I, the intensely shy.

A girl walks by – that's the one – and sits at a table. My choice. Not as nice as the rest. Much less so, in fact. What

she's lacking in lack of weight or in looks, for me is a plus 'cos
her type is unfussy by definition.

And so, I position myself nearby and give her the eye and
hope it'll be returned, that I won't be spurned with a sneer.

No fear. She's looking my way now, shyly, smiling coyly, the
moment highly charged, I must say and just may, when the
music slows, step up and propose she join me on the floor.

It does, I do – 'Hello' – and here we are now, holding each
other tightly, her heat against me, breasts and belly inflicting
upon me a fucking erection, so I imagine, as I always do, a
crew of woodlice; loathsome, heinous; crawling from the tip of
my penis. And like that, it wanes and wizens until it isn't a
problem any more.

Then, four or so songs on, they end the set and we sit and
chat. Her topic of conversation: how forsaken one can feel
sometimes, how left behind. And I find myself agreeing,
seeing I'm in the selfsame boat, you know? The both of us
solitary, pathetic and lonely, only not tonight because now
she's inviting me back to her abode for tea, which might be
code for a bit of gee. **"**

Vernon God Little
DBC Pierre, adapted by Tanya Ronder

☞ **WHO** Vernon, fifteen, a schoolboy from Texas.

☞ **TO WHOM** His mother.

☞ **WHERE** Somewhere between a courtroom and a cell on death row.

☞ **WHEN** Present day.

☞ **WHAT HAS JUST HAPPENED** Set in a small town in Texas, the play tells the story of fifteen-year-old schoolboy Vernon Little. At the time his best friend Jesus Navarro went on the rampage, massacring sixteen of their classmates before turning the gun on himself, Vernon, who suffers from unpredictable bowel movements, was outside the school grounds involuntarily defecating. However, when he is later found with Jesus's bag of ammunition in his hands, he is wrongly assumed to have been the accomplice. The town want someone to pay for the shootings, and Vernon becomes the scapegoat. He is accused of the murders. He goes on the run, and, in a crazed sequence of events that leads Vernon to Mexico, he is finally captured and found guilty of a crime he did not commit. Here, alone, somewhere between the courtroom and a cell on death row, Vernon talks to his mother. Although on stage with him, she is at home singing 'Please Help Me, I'm Falling' by Hank Locklin, so she does not hear him.

☞ **WHAT TO CONSIDER**

- The action is fast-paced. It has many twists and turns. Vernon encounters at least forty-five other characters during the course of the play. Read it to understand fully all that Vernon describes.

- This is the first time in the play that he is prepared to speak out. Up until now his embarrassment over his bowel movements has prevented him from doing so. However, here, nobody is listening.

- Vernon's mother is more concerned about the arrival of her new refrigerator than the plight of her son.

- The play's dark humour and absurd satirical nature.

- The play's heightened theatricality. Its use of music, song and dance.

- The kind of American culture that seeks to turn any event into a source of entertainment. Later in the play, a TV show asks viewers to vote for which criminal on death row they want to see exterminated first.

- The play is an adaptation of DBC Pierre's Booker Prize-winning novel.

- 'Jesus' is a Mexican/Spanish name and pronounced 'Hey-zoos', rather than the English 'Je-zus'.

☞ WHAT HE WANTS

- To prove his innocence.

- To confront his mother.

- To reveal the truth about the way in which his father died.

- His mother's love.

- Justice.

☞ KEYWORDS   storm   breaking   wired   jackknifed   shit   innocent

Vernon

❝ The way he ran from class, I knew the storm was breaking in Jesus. He'd been wired for weeks, more ditzy than usual, calling it love but not saying who with… If you'd come to Houston, Mom, and been in court you'd have heard about the photo on the Doctor's website. That morning in math, this picture of Jesus in these stupid panties, was on every computer in the room. 'Bambi Boy Butt Bazaar'? He had no idea. He jackknifed. I asked Lori to cover for me because I knew where he was headed. I raced to Keeter's on my bike, to

the den, where both our daddy's guns were. He wasn't there.
The den was locked, my key at home. I saw through the crack
in the door, Daddy's rifle was there, not moved since the day
we left it, but his daddy's had gone. My turn to jackknife.
Back on the bike, my insides cramped, what a surprise.
Gastro-enteritis fuckin' Little. I squatted, emptied my lower
tracts like rats from an airplane, right beside the den. '*Tell
them about the poo-poos!*' says my attorney, and he's right.
They'd know I wasn't in school, then. You'd know I wasn't in
school too, but what am I supposed to say? 'Sure, there's the
shit, right beside my papa's grave where me an' Mom buried
him in the middle of the fucking night after she shot him
dead. And in case you're interested, the gun's right behind
that corrugated door. The key? Sure – little box in my room –
anything else I can help with?' My shit makes me innocent but
it sure as hell would put you away. Seventeen children? How
could you think I did that?

By the time I cleaned myself up, Jesus was at school with his
pop's loaded rifle. I didn't get there in time. I found his bag
outside the classroom, picked it up, held on to it. Inside was
another round of ammunition beside his lunch – shrimp-paste
on white. I looked through the door and there they all were –
shot to pieces, and there was my goofy friend Jesus, with the
gun pointing deep inside his mouth. **99**

Voices from the Mosque*

Alecky Blythe

☞ **WHO**   Teenage Muslim.

☞ **TO WHOM**   The audience (see note on 'Direct audience address' in the introduction).

☞ **WHERE**   A London mosque.

☞ **WHEN**   Post-11th September 2001.

☞ **WHAT HAS JUST HAPPENED**   The play is made up of four short monologues in which three Muslim men talk about the after-effects of 9/11. The script has been created from real-life interviews, which were then edited. The play is one of twenty that make up a larger performance piece called *Decade*.

☞ **WHAT TO CONSIDER**

- In the original production, the text was fed to the actors through earphones. They did not learn their lines, but repeated exactly what they heard using the same intonation and hesitation, including coughs and any stutters.

- Take this as a note to keep your performance very real and spontaneous.

☞ **WHAT HE WANTS**

- To explain that Islam is a peaceful religion.

- To show that not all Muslims are terrorists.

- To defend himself against discrimination.

☞ **KEYWORDS**   discrimination   Islam   non-Muslim   terrorist   invade   rapes   kill/kills   defending   home   terrorises   peace   intimidated   love   life   jeopardise

* Published in the volume *Decade*

Teenage Muslim

❝ We weren't seen like that before s'like there was no discrimination ya know, way before (*Beat.*) two thousand and one ya know. Since then it's like when you hear Islam – or a non–Muslim would hear Islam will think terrorist straight away and a terrorist is a person that comes to invade your land, takes over, ya know, rapes your women, kills your people. That's what a terrorist is basically that terrorises your whole – area right? – And Muslims are not terrorists. We're not terrorists ya know. They're going to kill the brothers and sisters in Iraq an that yeah basically they're defending their home. The word Islam means peace and it's a peaceful religion – it's very beautiful. (*Beat.*)

I go on the-on the train, people are watching me. They're – especially if I'm wearing that long dress. I've 'ad to tell people 'what the *fuck* you lookin at?' literally because it in*tim*idated me. I *am* a human bein – (*Beat.*) ya know. Peo – I've been intimidated by people where they've been looking at me like – 'Terrorist' ya know, people holding onto their bags ya know. I-I don't like these things. I might be on the train – It doesn't mean every person wearing that long dress that goes on the train is a bomber. Ya know what I'm tryin a say? I'm against these things. I – Ya know I actually love my life more than anything. I love my life, I'm not going to jeopardise my life for anybody else. Unless it's do with my mum, my sister, my family *only*. Nobody else – no one is worth it ya know. But – a lot of discrimination has been happening (*Beat.*) in England (*Beat.*) towards Muslims – definitely – a hundred per cent. **❞**

What We Know

Pamela Carter

☞ **WHO**   Teenager, Scottish.

☞ **TO WHOM**   Lucy.

☞ **WHERE**   Lucy's kitchen.

☞ **WHEN**   Present day.

☞ **WHAT HAS JUST HAPPENED**   Lucy has been preparing a meal with her partner Jo. As they are cooking, Jo, 'as if by magic', mysteriously disappears and moments later a teenage boy appears from nowhere. Lucy has never met the boy. He says his name is Lee and then jokes that he is also called Hank and sometimes Marvin as in starving Marvin. He is hungry, and Laura makes him a cheese sandwich. He tells her he is here to help. When she questions him about his name, he does not answer but asks her if she has ever seen a dead body. The following speech is made up of their conversation.

☞ **WHAT TO CONSIDER**

- What started out as an ordinary evening soon takes a surreal turn as Lucy is forced to recall Jo's death.

- Lucy asks the teenager, 'why did you tell me that?' He replies, 'just a bit of banter. just making conversation. you gave me cheese so i thought maybe i should like say something. thought you might want to hear a story.'

- Lucy asks, 'where did you come from?' He replies, 'i dunno, the fairies left me?'

- Make a decision about what the sudden presence of the teenager might signify.

- The boy says that he is an honest person and that he always tells the truth.

- Note how the playwright has chosen to write solely in lower-case letters.

☞ **WHAT HE WANTS**

- To make conversation.
- To offer Lucy company in return for her feeding him.
- To share his sense of wonder at what he saw.

☞ **KEYWORDS** massive   random   radical   same – different
freaky   woooo, oooooop, waaaaay   wild   cool   sick
extreme   awesome

Teenager

❝ you ever seen a dead body? […] i saw a dead body once.

[…] it was years ago back when i was young, right? and i'm
playing out in these fields. and there's this stream with a pond,
like, and a big pipe across it you can stand on. really big.
massive.

so i'm sat up on this pipe and checking out the view. you
know, sun's shining, sky's blue. and i'm looking in the pond,
right?

[…]

cos people chuck random stuff in there or there are animals or
cars, you know, and it's interesting. but sometimes no and it's
just rubbish and so i'm having a butcher's and i see this
dummy, you know? like a dummy from a shop. and i think 'oh
look, someone's thrown a dummy in here.'

but then, there's this moment, right? really radical. […] you
know, when you look at something and it's one thing and then
you're still looking at it and it's not that thing any more; it's
the same but then it's totally different? same – different. same
– different. you with me?

[…] so one minute i'm looking at a dummy like from a shop,
you know. and the next minute, it's a woman.

a real woman. a real dead woman. […] and it's really freaky,
man, because I know that she's like dead just like in a film. and

it's not a film because it's real but it is like a film because everything's a bit slow-motion-y and a bit woooo.

it's like i'm a camera and i'm zooming in and out, you know, on this dead woman. like she's getting bigger and then smaller. close up and then far away, you know. oooooop and then waaaaay. do you know what i'm saying?

[...]

it's wild cos like i can do it now. like the whole thing's like my own personal film in my own head and i can like freeze it and go 'oooooop' and then 'waaaaay'. in my own head. well cool.

well, not for her. cos she was dead. it wasn't cool for her or anything, obviously. because that would be sick, like. not right.

[...]

extreme stuff. awesome. **99**

The Winterling

Jez Butterworth

☞ **WHO**   Patsy, twenty-five, gang member, Londoner.

☞ **TO WHOM**   West and Wally, both in their forties, gang members.

☞ **WHERE**   A derelict farmhouse, Dartmoor.

☞ **WHEN**   Present day.

☞ **WHAT HAS JUST HAPPENED**   Wally and Patsy, both gang members from London, have arrived at the deserted farmhouse in the middle of Dartmoor. It is night-time in the winter. They have come to see Len West, a former gang member. Patsy, who has never met Len, is introduced as Wally's stepson. Wally is going out with Rita, Patsy's mother. Patsy is convinced that Len West has 'raised an eyebrow' at this news and has therefore disrespected his mother. Before he can say anything, Wally sends Patsy back out to the car to retrieve his cigarettes. On his return, Patsy is still upset. He confronts Len about how he believes he 'Expressed a degree of astonishment… that Wally here would be emotionally or otherwise associated with someone like Mum, like my mother. Like Rita.' The speech that follows is his attempt to explain the relationship.

☞ **WHAT TO CONSIDER**

- Throughout the play there is a sense of menace.

- Characters are volatile. We are never quite sure where their loyalties lie. Here, for instance, we do not know whether Patsy wants to attack West or in some strange way befriend him. In any event, the speech acts as a kind of warning.

- Patsy has no idea why he and Wally are there. He got a call to meet with Wally at 10 p.m. outside Costcutters. They have driven through the night to get to the farm, but Wally is refusing to explain. Read the play to discover what Wally is intending.

- The 'Lamberts' are Wally's cigarettes that Patsy has had to retrieve from the car.

- Decide to what extent Patsy is embellishing the truth.

☞ WHAT HE WANTS

- To defend his mother. (Although there is a cruelty in the way that he too describes her, blood is thicker than water.)

- To assert himself with the two older men. He has been undermined by Wally when he was sent out to the car.

- To unnerve both Wally and West.

☞ KEYWORDS   good   die   rot   kind   strong   angel   cold
nightmarish   ogre   bully   vicious   bitter   love   bent/benders

Patsy

❝ Can I tell you a quick story, Mr West? The other day, I'm back home at my old mum's. I'm in the tub, when the front door opens and in comes Wally, with Mum. They've been out, they're a bit tiddly, in the hall. I'm in the tub. They don't know I'm there. (*Beat.*) Wally says, I heard him downstairs clear as a bell, he says, 'Rita, you are a good good woman. Without you, I'm nothing. I'm just another stupid old saggy dog that's going to die, rot and be forgotten.'[…] And she says, 'Bollocks, Wally, you are an amazing human being. You are a kind, strong, many-faceted individual, who inspires and nourishes each soul you touch.' And Wally goes up. Big heaving sobs. He says, 'Rita, you are an angel sent to protect me. It's cold out there. It's cold. Hold me. Please hold me.' (*Beat.*) Now, to imagine this story, you have to bear in mind since you last seen Rita she's got new teeth. And she don't drink shorts no more. She's got the teeth, some eyebrow lift what never come off. New set of Bristols. Wally stumped for 'em. Don't get me wrong. Still, Rita emphatically does not scrub up. She's still got the sideburns. The shoulders. The big goalie hands. Plus, no amount of sawing and stitching and hammering is going to change what's underneath. Time spent with Rita still often has a nightmarish quality. Wally's had to slap her down once or twice in public. It's worked wonders.

She's made him look a right prat once or twice. A proper
clown. And you've always got to watch her. She'll go off like a
rucksack. You can't give her a yard. Turn your back for one
minute, she's in the bucket cupboard with a broom across the
door. In that Chinese restaurant. With half the staff. About
sixteen Chinamen in a broom cupboard. They should have
rung Roy Castle. But then Wally's no church picnic. Ask the
birds. Proper ogre, once the door's shut. Right bedroom bully,
once the light's off. So what I'm saying is, I understand your
reaction, Mr West. But whereas most people would agree with
us, whereas most people agree Rita's a vicious, bitter moo you
wouldn't pork with a spacesuit on, Wally here don't share the
public's qualms. And the best bit, the bonus, is I get to spend
time with Wally. And time spent with Wally is golf, mate. It's
pure golf. On the way over here, he's pulled the car over, he
looked me in the eye and he's said, 'I don't want you to think
I'm soppy. I'm not being bent or nothing but I love you,
Patsy.' […] 'I do. And I'll look after you.' […] 'And I'm not
being bent, but I love that Mr West. That Len – ' he said.
Look. He's blushing now, like a woman, like a prat, but he said
it, on the M5. 'It don't matter what he's done. Why he's out in
the cold. I'd go to the Moon for that man. To the Moon.'
(*Beat.*) I just want to say… Thank you, Wally. Some fathers
wouldn't. Some would just leave you in the dark. Not you,
Wally. And also to say, and *I'm* not being bent, but ditto. I love
you too. And you love Mr West. And Mr West, I don't doubt,
you know, eh? Eh? I bet? Eh? You know? Eh? So here we are.
Eh? Men who love each other, but who are not benders.
Here's your Lamberts, Wally. **"**